PRAISE FOR *THE PHENOMENON*

"In his surprisingly open and compelling memoir—a standout in the motley genre of athlete autobiographies—Ankiel details his many efforts to cope with the problem, from drinking to drugs to a brief retirement to deciding that he'd rather forget pitching altogether, returning as a hitter and an outfielder instead."

—*Atlantic*

"This book is a moving read as Ankiel bares his soul and provides the reader with an intimate look at the psychological unraveling he experienced. . . . To throw in a baseball cliché, Ankiel left it all on the field with this book. Don't miss it."

—*Washington Times*

"I strongly recommend this book. I'm a sucker for happy endings, and this isn't your classic happy ending. But Ankiel the hitter, and Ankiel in his post-career world, and Ankiel the dad breaking the chain with his own father is one redemptive story."

—Peter King, *Sports Illustrated*

"For those interested in the psychology of baseball, Ankiel's book bats close to .400."

—*St. Louis Dispatch*

"What happened to Rick Ankiel is one of the more remarkable stories in baseball history. . . . This riveting story will make you feel Ankiel's anxiety about battling this mysterious affliction."

—*Chicago Tribune*

"It's a much-needed narrative in the sports memoir genre, one that tackles the topic of mental health, something only a few books before it have done."

—*Literary Hub*

"Ankiel's battle with this mysterious mental block and his decision to remake his baseball career as an outfielder is told in *The Phenomenon*, an out-of-the-ordinary story of baseball courage and determination."

—*Christian Science Monitor*

"A former Major League Baseball player offers an affecting account of his unique professional career and dramatic personal life. Most baseball memoirs hold little appeal for readers who are not already devoted fans. With assistance from sports journalist [Tim] Brown (coauthor with Jim Abbott of *Imperfect: An Improbable Life*, 2012), Ankiel offers more. . . . A solid sports memoir that explores more than just sports."

—*Kirkus Reviews*

"Revealing, vulnerable, and triumphant, Rick Ankiel and Tim Brown provide a poignant reminder in this age of statistics- and computer-driven analysis that it is real people who play the game. Real people, carrying family history, huge expectations, and lifelong dreams along for the ride. This book will change how you watch the game and those who play it."

—Jim Abbott, former MLB pitcher and bestselling
author of *Imperfect*

"Each year lots of baseball books roll off the presses. Some are very good, a few are extraordinary. Rick Ankiel's memoir falls into the second category. A story of rare promise and bewildering pain. The heartbreak, the humiliation, and the high points—fewer than expected, but memorable still. All told with honesty, humility, empathy, and an eye for telling detail. A winding and often bumpy road that ends with perhaps that best of victories—good-natured acceptance and the personal understanding and insight that goes with it."

—Bob Costas

"In Tim Brown's expert hands, Rick Ankiel's journey is heart-breaking, unsentimental, and, in an entirely unexpected way, victorious. A superb book not just about the glory of baseball, but about how we repair ourselves."

> —Mark Kriegel, author of *Namath*, *Pistol*, and *The Good Son*

"Rick Ankiel has always been a true phenomenon. He had phenomenal talent, and when he faced hardship, he proved he had phenomenal character too. His book is a candid and powerful story of his pitching success, his cruel and dramatic career derailment, and his historic resurrection as a power-hitting outfielder. Your lasting impression is of Rick the winner and champion husband, father, and person, with a story that impacts us all."

> —Tony La Russa, Hall of Fame manager

"Many of us took one look at Rick Ankiel's extraordinary athletic gifts and figured that he had it made. But his great talent did not account for the inexplicable demons that he had to endure, from an abusive home to a career-altering mystery. *The Phenomenon* is bravely candid about his challenges in life and his journey through a game that humbles all of us."

> —Hall of Famer Joe Torre, four-time World Series Championship manager and MLB's chief baseball officer

"A great story of a young man's ability to persist in the face of complicated and difficult issues—I admire him for it and the success he eventually achieved."

> —Bill Parcells, Hall of Fame NFL coach

"*The Phenomenon* is a must-read for anyone who has wrestled with his own demons—which is everyone. I couldn't put this book down, maybe because I knew parts of the story, but more likely because it displays the power of the human spirit to overcome the odds."

> —Mike Matheny, manager of the St. Louis Cardinals

THE PHENOMENON

Pressure, the Yips,
and the Pitch
that Changed My Life

THE
PHENOM
ENON

RICK ANKIEL
and Tim Brown

PublicAffairs
New York

PublicAffairs

Hachette Book Group

1290 Avenue of the Americas, New York, NY 10104

www.publicaffairsbooks.com

@Public_Affairs

Printed in the United States of America

First Trade Paperback Edition: April 2018

Published by PublicAffairs, an imprint of Perseus Books, LLC, a subsidiary of Hachette Book Group, Inc. The PublicAffairs name and logo is a trademark of the Hachette Book Group.

The Hachette Speakers Bureau provides a wide range of authors for speaking events. To find out more, go to www.hachettespeakersbureau.com or call (866) 376-6591.

The publisher is not responsible for websites (or their content) that are not owned by the publisher.

Print book interior design by Amy Quinn

Library of Congress Cataloging-in-Publication Data

Names: Ankiel, Rick.
Title: The phenomenon : pressure, the yips, and the pitch that changed my life / Rick Ankiel.
Description: 1 | New York : PublicAffairs, 2017.
Identifiers: LCCN 2016050707 | ISBN 9781610396868 (hardback)
Subjects: LCSH: Abbott, Jim, 1967- | Pitchers (Baseball)—United States--Biography. | Baseball players--United States--Biography. | BISAC: BIOGRAPHY & AUTOBIOG-RAPHY / Sports. | SPORTS & RECREATION / Baseball / Essays & Writings. | SELF-HELP / Motivational & Inspirational.
Classification: LCC GV865.A495 A3 2017 | DDC 796.357092 [B] --dc23 LC record available at https://lccn.loc.gov/2016050707

ISBN: 978-1-5417-7365-3 (paperback)

ISBN: 978-1-61039-687-5 (e-book)

LSC-C

10 9 8 7 6 5 4 3 2 1

Rick:

To my wife, Lory, who helped me to love and trust again.

To my sons, Declan and Ryker: You have brought me so much happiness. In your lives you will encounter bumps in the road. I hope this book reminds you to never give up. I love you.

To Harvey: with your love and guidance, here's what I did about it.

Tim:

For Kelly. And for Connor and Timmy.

INTRODUCTION

I have two sons. They give me a chance to be good. To be present. To be better.

Their names are Declan and Ryker. They fish with me, like I fished with my father. He was a great fisherman, near as I remember. Probably still is.

They like baseball enough. I loved baseball for a while, then wasn't so sure, then loved it again. Baseball was who I was for a very long time, for better or worse. I'd still recommend it to them, if they were to ask, and it seems they're getting old enough to start asking. They're free to decide for themselves. In the meantime, I'll throw them all the batting practice they want, as long as they promise to be patient and wear a helmet.

They are so young, at ages I barely remember. They're good boys. They generally mind their mother—my wife,

Lory—who occasionally must believe she has three boys instead of two. There might be something to that, me taking a do-over on the childhood thing. Part of me wants a second one that I'll recall with more clarity and warmth.

I think all the time about raising two boys, about being good at something as important as being a father. I think about it when they're laughing at the same goofy joke that makes me laugh, and when they cry on a day when I'm sad too, and when we're just driving down the road in my pickup truck singing along to Luke Bryan.

Maybe they're missing a tooth that day, their hair's all crazy, and they've half a chocolate doughnut stuck to their faces, and it makes me wonder how they ever got so perfect. It makes me wonder if I was ever one of those kids in that rearview mirror, strapped into their seats, so sure that today will be great, that tomorrow will be too, that Mom and Dad will be together forever, and that I'll be there for them forever too.

Declan is five. He likes math, and he sometimes kills time by practicing his ABCs, humming the alphabet song while he's turning Lego blocks into cars and houses and things only he recognizes. He watches *American Ninja Warrior* on television. He looks like me. We have the same eyes, my grandfather's eyes. When he was born, the nurse bundled him in a blue blanket and set him in my arms, and he was the most beautiful thing I'd ever seen. He blinked up at me, his father, the man who would, I promised, be kind to him forever, and teach him to be kind to others, and love him and try never to disappoint him. I would not call him names. I would not abuse his mother.

I would stand behind him when he needed a push, before him when he needed a shield, beside him when he did not. He was the next generation, different than the last. Better, I promised, for Declan, my first. He bats and throws left-handed, like me.

Ryker is four. He already understands that as the youngest and smallest in the house, he has to be tougher, feistier, and a little more clever than his brother. He is my firecracker. On first reference lately he'll answer to "Hot Sauce." He also likes whatever Declan likes that day, which seems to be his strategy to get under Declan's skin. Ryker is a right-hander. He also came in a blue blanket, and with the same promises.

We watch baseball when it's on at night.

"Who are we rooting for, Papa?" Declan asks.

Well, I say, Papa played with him, and he's nice, so we'll root for them tonight. Or, Papa hit a few homers and won some games for that team once, the one wearing red, so we'll hope they win tonight. In the meantime, I'll put Cardinals hats on them and tell them why later. For a few hours we'll talk about the game and the men who play it, why they play it, and how they got there. We'll high-five the good stuff and try to ignore the losses and make plans to be back on the couch tomorrow night, maybe for more living-room Wiffle Ball. Anything off the chandelier is a home run. Their curiosity about baseball has drawn me back in. Not that I didn't like it. But there was always something else to do—a tiny car to race around the carpet, dinner to eat and baths to take and teeth to brush and a book to read aloud before their breaths would become long and steady and perfect. There were road trips and new teams in new cities and short conversations on the phone when I told them I loved them and would see them soon—"Home in two sleeps," I'd say—and, yeah, I'd try to hit them a home run tonight. Now we do baseball together, and it's uncomplicated.

Some evenings we'll gather up the fishing gear and carry it to the dock off the backyard. There are snapper and catfish and snook hiding in those depths. The sun's setting and the air's cooler and whatever's left over from dinner might be on our hooks. You'd be amazed at what a hunk of chicken nugget will bring. In a half whisper, I'll tell them what my father told me about how smart those fish are, and what they're hungry for, and when. How they seem to know what's coming. The boys are sometimes more interested in the bait bucket, where sardines or greenies or goggle-eyes or mullets await their turn on the hook, just as I was at their age. I find myself hoping they love this, the hunt, the wins and losses, the beauty of it all, because I love it so much, and because a father and his boys ought to be able to do this together forever.

Some nights, when the water is calm and the lines are taut, they look at me in a way I've never looked at myself. Maybe I'm imagining that. But I like the way it feels. I like what it has taught me about selflessness and accountability. About showing up. I like what it has taught me about myself and what I need to be today and every day after that.

See, there is the life you want. There is the life you get. There is what you do with that.

Simple, only not.

I had what they called a generational left arm, and I knew it from the time I was barely older than Declan. There are plenty of good arms in baseball. There are great arms. There are a few—very few—special arms. I had one of those. The scouts said so. The batters said so. Everyone said so. I couldn't help but believe them. I wanted to be special.

That was the life I had, the one I'd live through that special arm. Until it wasn't. Mine is the story of what I did with that.

It is the story of a childhood that could not be trusted because of a father who could not be trusted, and the story of the arm that carried me away from years of snarling abuse. I was in the major leagues barely two years out of high school, a big leaguer and celebrated phenomenon— that word—at twenty, and at twenty-one the starting pitcher in the biggest game of the only life I ever wanted.

It is the story of what happened after that. For on that very day, when I asked my arm to be more special than ever, it deserted me. Maybe I deserted it. For the next five years, I chased the life I wanted, the one I believed I owed to myself, the one I probably believed the world owed to me. To the gift that was my left arm. To the work I'd done to help make it special. To the life I thought I deserved.

My father watched from prison. I was glad for that. I was especially glad for my mother.

It is the story of my fight to return to the pitcher I was, a fight mounted on a psyche—a will—formed as protection against my own father. There were small victories. There were far more failures. Those pushed me deeper into my own mind, into the dark fight-or-flight corners where the costs in happiness and emotional stability were severe. The fights of my childhood against a drunken, raging father had tracked me into manhood, and now the villain was within me, restless and relentless and just out of reach. For the life I wanted, I thrashed savagely and bled freely. There is a saying that goes loosely like this: Don't fight the man who does not mind what he looks like when the fight is over. There is no winning that fight. That fight never ends. I stood in for five years, then fought some more. I wish I could have said at the end, "Yeah, but you should've seen the other guy." But when I got done fighting, he looked fine. He wasn't even breathing hard.

It is the story of some triumph. Maybe I would not be a pitcher, and certainly I would not be the pitcher who had walked to the mound one afternoon in St. Louis a long time before and staggered off. Instead, I would be a ballplayer.

I would start again in my midtwenties, ancient for the lower minor leagues, and I would return to the major leagues on a midsummer night in 2007 as an outfielder— an unfathomable journey even for me, the guy who'd trudged every inch of it—and I would play the game against the backdrop of the life I'd always wanted while living the life I got.

They called me "the Natural." It never felt that easy. It never felt that pretty. But I loved the story. If there was a comparison to be drawn, I guess I'd be closer to the Roy Hobbs in the book, the one Bernard Malamud wrote, a grittier version of the Roy Hobbs that showed up thirty-two years later in movie theaters. I had a past I didn't quite know how to explain, and had no desire to. It was too dark in there. It was too personal. Nobody needed to know but me, and I'd already spent too many nights trying to forget.

When the time came, be it on the pitcher's mound or in the batter's box, I would face the game alone. Just me and the demons. They'd threatened to wreck my career, as they had the careers of plenty before me. And every day I returned to test the demons again. I'd take one more breath, throw one more pitch, leave it behind, and try again. When there were no more pitches in me, so little hope left in me, I changed my spikes, picked up a bat, took one more breath, took one more swing, and tried again. Mine is the story of the making of a big leaguer, which isn't so unusual. Except I did it twice. It is the story of the making of the man, the best I could make him. Once.

It is the story of relationships. A boy and his volatile father. A boy and his abused mother. A boy and the game that summoned him. A young man and his conscience. And then a man lost, and those who would help him win back the life he wanted or make do with the life he got.

It is about the relationship between a boy and the game that freed him, and then turned on him, and why.

And it is a story about how a brain can take the simplest task—pick up that baseball and throw it there—and make it near impossible. How men like me, big, strong men—major-league pitchers and catchers, NBA shooters, NFL quarterbacks, pro golfers—can be reduced to somber, anxiety-ridden casualties of the mind. In the grasp of my monster, I would wake nightly soaked in sweat and terror. And then I would begin the slow daily preparation to return to a baseball clubhouse, where I would change into a uniform, snatch a glove from the bottom of my locker, and wonder if today—finally today—would be the day I would be me again.

For the longest time, I didn't much care why it was that I was the one who had been flattened, that there were a million pitchers out there and I had to be the one who was the sweaty, lost, breathless mess. Would it have changed anything to know why? Would it have made me a better pitcher? Would it have gotten me back my life?

If a tire goes flat, does the reason change anything? You go to the trunk, drag out the spare, jack up the car, and keep going. The road is still there. The clock is still ticking. The destination remains. A hundred cars pass in the meantime, and the people inside think the same thing: "Better him than me." They think, "Poor guy. Now, do I take this left or the next one?" They think, "Looks cold out there."

I didn't need them. I could change my own tire. I could fill it with air and go as long as I could and fill it again and keep going and fill it again and make it another mile.

Then, years later, with all that road behind me, two separate baseball careers behind me, I did begin to wonder what that was all about. My sons would want to know. The next generation of ballplayers, who would stop along their roads for them? Who would stand before them, arms crossed, squinting into the sun, and say, "Welp, looks like you picked up a nail. Happened to me once too."

I could help, maybe. I could care, for sure. They would know they were not alone, and even if that tire wouldn't ever be quite right again, and it probably wouldn't, at least somebody who'd been right there before had stopped. I was finally ready to know more, to ask around, to hear their stories, to learn what had happened to me. The symptoms I knew. The cause, though? I wanted to ask, not in a pained, pathetic way but in a clinical way: Why me? And, then, who's next? What's next?

My story is a trip back along that road, only this time with my head up, curious, honest, looking back over the lives that I wanted and got, and the time I shared a brain with a monster. It's still in there somewhere. We learned to live with each other. Perhaps we could ally against the monsters in other people's heads. In that, I wanted to look ahead too. I wanted to travel that road with Lory at my side and my sons strapped into the backseat. I would be present. I would be better.

On the very first day, standing on a pitcher's mound in St. Louis, I could hear the blood draining from my head. On many in between, I cursed it, medicated it, drank with it, and pleaded with it. On the very last day, I surrendered to it, stepped around it, and chose to live with it. For that, I would win, dammit, I would win, and so years later, maybe my sons would too. We get what we get sometimes, and it's still worth a fight. Every bit of it.

I want them to know my story when they are old enough and curious enough, which is what this book is for. I didn't want to leave anything out because some of it was great, everything I'd ever wanted, and some of it was not, and they should know that. It's their road too. Maybe I could clear some of the nails.

See, there's only so much you can remember over a fishing hole. There's only so much worth remembering.

CHAPTER
ONE

The warning would come as something more than a drizzle, more like a rush of water across a rocky bed, a creek rising but in the distance, over the next rise, maybe beyond that. I'd be safe, wouldn't I? If I didn't move, if I stayed away, looked away, it would pass. I'd breathe again. My heart, my heart would want to race off, to take me with it.

C'mon, Rick, we gotta go. We gotta go now.

But I couldn't run. I had to stay. And it was coming for me. It always came for me.

Fight it, Rick. Fight it. C'mon, Rick, remember your mechanics. Right foot back . . .

The clatter would swell, an off-key orchestra finding its full throat, its vibrations leaking into the room. Then flooding the room, the sound of blood draining from my head, leaking through my veins, sloshing through my arteries, pooling and spilling and splashing, cold and fast like rainwater through a tin downspout, a rowboat taking on seawater. The louder the roar, the harder my heart hammered and the freer the blood ran, behind my forehead, past my eyes and ears and through my cheeks, along the back of my neck.

Colors faded. A sweat rose, but I was chilled. My mouth ached for water. I couldn't feel my hands. My eyes followed the length of my left arm, searching. I was supposed to be holding something. A baseball. Was I holding the baseball? Had they thrown it back?

It was too loud. All those people, they'd be shouting at me, for me, and what I would hear was coming from some darkness within, from inside my head. The rushing noise was coming. I was alone.

C'mon, Rick, play the game. You know how.

But I didn't know how. I did once. I'd forgotten.

Dammit, Rick, throw the ball. Right foot back . . .

It was there, in my hand. I could see it. I could not feel it. Not the seams or the muddied cowhide or the roundness of it or the weight of it. Not the familiarity of it. Like I was wearing oven mitts. Like somebody else was holding the ball for me, offering it, waiting for me to reach out.

Take the ball, Rick. Take the ball and throw it.

It had me. It had me again.

It gathered, something horrible and tireless, leaving me light-headed and unsure and blinded. Defenseless. So completely defenseless. I'd laugh it off, cry it out, throw until I couldn't anymore. I'd leave it alone, try to forget, just for an hour or two, maybe a day, then come back and find it was worse—deeper in me—than before.

I was a young man, barely old enough to sip a beer, now in dire need of one or six. I threw a pitch, it staggered to the backstop, and everything changed. My head opened up and filled with uncertainty. My body shut down. Panic thickened my throat. My career stumbled off with a single wayward pitch and took parts of my life with it, parts I loved and parts I hated and parts I'd not even known were there. Anxiety came like a dam break, and then I was wading in it, one sodden step at a time, sloshing about and slowly . . . slowly . . . drowning in it.

I could throw a ball once. I could pitch. Man, could I pitch. And then I couldn't. I didn't know why I couldn't. More than a decade later, I don't know why I couldn't.

They said I was the next Sandy Koufax, he being the greatest left-hander to ever grip a baseball. Then I wasn't.

I'd known where my life was headed, at least where I expected it to be headed, and then I didn't.

I'd known where the fight was because it was in front of me, usually sixty feet, six inches away, precisely that distance. Sometimes, in my youth, the fight had been closer, much closer, with wild eyes and boozy breath and a bear-trap temper. Those weren't the real fights, though. Those would come later, and they would be everywhere, and no-where, and merciless, when the boggy anxiety would rise and I couldn't hear fifty thousand people screaming over the racket in my own head. I wouldn't win. I'd lose and fall deeper, farther into the darkness, where the air thinned and the simplest act—throwing a baseball—became a test of my manhood. And my resolve. My goddamned sanity.

A standard major-league pitcher's mound is ten inches tall—just high enough to afflict me with baseball's version of altitude poisoning.

In the middle of it, a man at Shea Stadium held up a handmade sign. There were thousands of people up there, and the month was October, so the place was loud and edgy, as New York could be. It seemed they were all yelling at me, drawing out the final syllable. "You suck, An-*keeeel*!" "You're a freak, An-*keeeel*!" "Mix in a strike, An-*keeeel*!" I never, ever looked up into the crowd in those moments. I was tougher than that. I was too sure of myself. Those people couldn't touch me. This time I looked up.

My career was coming apart. My team could not rely on me. I hadn't slept in days. My father was in jail and calling me at all hours, pulling me backward again. My mother kept asking if I was, you know, all right, like maybe I'd contracted some unspeakable neuromuscular condition from the dugout floor. Reporters chased me with questions I could not answer. Nobody could. People—friends, even—would simply stare, which was bad enough. Others would say kind things, encouraging things, but they didn't know, and it felt like pity, and that I could not endure.

What could a few thousand strangers say that I didn't already know?

So I looked up.

Above the grinning man, atop arms extended like a *V*, the sign announced, "Ankiel is an X-file."

He had no idea. None of them did.

People were watching, so I laughed. But that was a lie.

You should know, perhaps, that I won in the end, or felt as though I did. I surrendered finally and chose a new fight, one that didn't spawn ritual nightmares, or chase me into a vodka bottle, or have me counting breaths backward from one hundred to one, then starting over, all day long, just to make it to game time, just to have my mind right, only to have it all fall apart anyway.

That was the lousy part, and that's a significant part of the story, how it began on an otherwise perfect afternoon at a ballpark in St. Louis, where the game is religion and the players its dutiful and celebrated servants. Unless one were to, say, wear the Cardinals' sacred colors and stand in the middle of an event known as game one of the playoffs and commence to throw pitch after pitch to the backstop.

That was eleven days before the guy with the sign sought entry into my psyche and before at least a dozen pitches that might as well have been sprayed from an untended fire hose. If he'd really wanted inside my head, he would have needed an affinity for crowds—there was a lot going on in there.

Still short of my prime, and bulletproof, and just then coming upon manhood, still out in front of all that pursued me, I would not be great, not in the way anyone might have foretold. I should have pitched forever.

I didn't pitch forever. I never really pitched again. I survived for a while, just barely. I told myself I was pitching, and that would have to do.

They call it "the Thing" because there's no diagnosis and no cure, and so they kick it around and try not to look at it and do not become so friendly as to actually give it a name because "anxiety disorder" is not the kind of phrase one slips into a baseball conversation. Just the Thing. Basically, it turns a regular guy with a physical gift into the jackknife in the corner surrounded by dog-eared self-help books, one eye on the clock, trying to get his head straight and nerves settled by game time.

I'd seen them before, the poor souls. And what I'd think was *Damn, man, get ahold of yourself and just throw the baseball.* Then the Thing came for me.

I swore it would not beat me. I'd worked too hard for too long to be anything other than the next Koufax, or the first Ankiel, or whatever was going to come of it. I would throw precise, relentless, plain mean fastballs past men who could do nothing about it. I would stand on a thousand more pitchers' mounds, grow old on them, and smart, and rich, and I would be special. I'd earned that. I would become what I'd dreamed myself becoming when I was a boy, when the car would pull into the driveway in the dead of night, and the front door would slam, and the shouting would start, and the violence would come, and I would have nowhere to go but a ball field on a summer's morning. That was the vision I'd sleep to, or try to, beneath the racket. I would take hold of whatever I came up against, and I would cast it aside and keep going, and I would put another mile between me and wherever my father was.

I would be better. I would win. I would be fearless.

But that was a lie.

Never would I understand if the Thing had simply happened upon me, or if I'd somehow summoned it in a particularly vulnerable patch, or if it had hunted me for years—waiting, plotting, and taking aim. It would not speak to me. It would not explain. What I knew was that it came for me. Just, it seemed in those lonely days, for me.

It would not drag me into my youth, into the terrible truth of where I'd been and what I'd seen and where I'd failed. But it did, because that was a lie too. Why hadn't I stood up to him? What kind of man—what kind of person—had I left back there? Who was I hiding?

Fifteen years later, I know where it sent me, and what it made of me, and most days I accept that. True, sometimes I wonder what would have come had the Thing never been, or if it had been coming for me all along and this was the life I was supposed to have instead of the one I made the best of. But not often anymore. See, I feel like I won. Like I found a cure. Not a cure, exactly; a way around it. All I had to do was look up. All I had to do was stop the fear from rising.

Take the ball, Rick. Take the ball and throw it.

"Ankiel is an X-file."

That's funny. Today, it is honestly funny.

This is why.

CHAPTER
TWO

It's a long story, really, about baseball and me, about baseball saving me and then leaving me on my own. It's about my father and me, I suppose. It's about the monster that came to get me, and a man named Harvey Dorfman and me against the monster, and how a monster built over a lifetime cannot be killed with a single pitch or a thousand or in a day or over a baseball season or maybe ever. It's about living with the shame of a monster that's big enough to fill the world and small enough to fit inside one's head, that's invisible and plain as a man's pitching line, that has no voice and yet screamed me awake in the night.

That's how I saw it. Of course, most of the time I was the only one who could, which was a relief and a curse. I lived with it, denied it, hid it, treated it, and swung swords at it until I couldn't.

Then morning would come, as would the new struggle, same as the old struggle.

The rest saw not the monster but its casualty, that being me and whatever shrapnel was in the box score. That's not to say I was an innocent bystander. It was my brain, after all. My body. My arm. My fear. It was mine to bear and so mine to slay. And, hell, at the end of the day it was just a baseball game, just . . . a . . . freakin' . . . baseball . . . game, that was all, and I'd shrug and smile and move along, except it meant everything to me and I didn't want to shrug or smile or move along. I wanted blood, which was life as both the monster and its casualty, and the blood that was shed was always mine.

Before that, I was a kid with a fastball, a curveball, a future, and a way of smirking at the world. It couldn't get to me. Nothing could. I'd already taken the world's best shot: my dad.

The monster—the yips, the Thing, the phenomenon; it had a few aliases—arrived on a Tuesday afternoon in October, the end of my rookie year. I'd made 30 major-league starts, won 11 of them, struck out 194 batters in 175 innings, was the winning pitcher in the game that clinched the National League Central Division title, and would be runner-up for National League Rookie of the Year. I felt like I was getting better as the season went on, thanks to Dave Duncan, the pitching coach, and Mike Matheny, the veteran catcher who could call a game and soothe a rookie's occasionally jumpy heartbeat. I even hit .250 with a couple home runs.

Then I had a bad day. A very bad day.

I was not hurt. I was not afraid. I was not sick or distracted or particularly anxious. There was no terrible accident. That said, days on ball fields generally don't come much worse. In game one of the National League Division Series, on a warm and sunny afternoon with a slight cross breeze, in front of exactly 52,378 people, including my mom, I stood on the mound at Busch Stadium, convinced I would be great. That it was my destiny.

And then I was not great. I don't know why. I only know what happened and what it did to me (or what I did to it, as I'm sure there's a conversation to be had about that), where it led me and where it left me.

The date was October 3, 2000, a box on a calendar page. Innocent enough. I was twenty-one years old and enjoying a life fresh to the big leagues.

I wasn't the trusting sort. My childhood had wrung that out of me. I wouldn't apologize for it. Hell, I was in some ways grateful for it, for the toughness it inspired. Nobody could touch me. But I had begun to feel like I belonged. I had begun to trust tomorrow.

These were the St. Louis Cardinals of Mark McGwire and Darryl Kile, of Jim Edmonds and Will Clark and J. D. Drew, and of Tony La Russa. To plenty in the ballpark that day, they remained the Cardinals of Bob Gibson, Stan Musial, Ozzie Smith, and Lou Brock. The Cardinals were hardball royalty.

But this day was to be mine. Game one, the Atlanta Braves in town, the Cardinals a generation removed from their last World Series title, a touch-the-sword-to-my-shoulder occasion. They'd give the ball to their future, to their present, and he—that being me—would oppose the masterful Greg Maddux. For hopeful Cardinals fans, the coming three hours were to preview the next twenty years.

Instead, I threw a pitch that missed the catcher's mitt, that didn't look like it should but did, and I wondered how that had happened, and I narrowed my eyes and clenched my jaw and threw another pitch, defiant, but it was already too late. In that moment, my career had ended, only without the compassion of old age or the finality of a blown shoulder, the way other careers end, and then without the benefit of a veteran's reflection. I would walk away humiliated. But that was a long way off, after I'd walked off dozens of ball fields, humiliated.

A single unremarkable pitch, one I'd thrown countless times before, would launch countless more pitches remarkable for how each drew me sixty feet, six inches closer to an inevitable and inglorious and sweat-stained end.

Maybe there'd be a thousand reasons for the pitch, why I threw it, how I threw it, how it ended up at the backstop, and why—even as it bounded away—I never could let it go. More, why it never would let go of me.

The forty-fourth pitch of the game. Third inning. One out. A one-strike count to Andruw Jones. Greg Maddux at first base. Cardinals 6, Braves 0. Throw strikes, keep the ball in the big part of the park, nothing crazy, we win. I win. The future wins.

The catcher was Carlos Hernández. He'd been around. Good guy. Solid backup. And not Mike Matheny, who'd sliced his hand with a hunting knife he'd received for his birthday about a week before. Mike had caught my games for most of the year, because I was a rookie who believed in every pitch Matheny ever called and every word he ever spoke. His voice was deep and possessed a low rattle, something like Clint Eastwood's, which was reassuring. Except now I was on the mound, and Dirty Harry was hanging over the dugout rail.

Hernández put two fingers down. A curveball. He leaned to his right, away from Jones, who batted right-handed and had hit thirty-six home runs in the regular season. Curveball away sounded good to me. I blinked my approval, came set over the rubber, let my eyes drift to Maddux at first base, then turned to narrow in on Hernández's mitt.

Everything was fine. I wasn't tired. Not too hot, not too cold. The crowd was into it, in a swirl of colors and clamor and belief in me and a six-run lead. Arm felt good. Strong. Head was clear. No thoughts of anything other than a curveball, so natural there'd be no need to consider the mechanics of it. Just let it go, hit the glove. Already I could see the path the ball would take when it left my hand, a moment's clarity, a promise of the future. For an instant a tunnel would form in my mind's eye. The ball would leave my hand, pass through that tunnel, and land with a *thwack*. That's what I saw. It's what I always saw. I took a breath, relaxed, felt the ball in my hand, the power in my legs, imagined the tunnel, and set about delivering that pitch.

I'd learned the basics of that curveball early in high school from an extremely patient pitching coach named Charlie Frazier, then honed it during tryouts and practices for the Junior Olympics in Joplin, Missouri. Bill Olson was the pitching coach. He'd kneel between the mound and the plate, and I'd throw dozens of curveballs over his head toward the catcher. "Nope," he'd say. "Nope. Nope. Pull down the shade. Nope. Wham, that's it! Throw another, just like it. Nope. Yes! There!" He'd turned my curveball from a flabby backyard ruse into a big-league weapon. I loved that pitch. I trusted it. And if it ever got sloppy I'd remember those days flipping curveballs over Bill Olson's head, the way he'd talk me through them inch by inch, how they felt so perfect out of my hand, until it was part of me again.

Then, I don't know. I held on to the ball too long. Tried not to hang the curveball. Didn't exactly trust it. Rushed it. Instead of flicking the outer inches of the strike zone, I launched the pitch too far right. It came out of my hand, off my fingers, all wrong. Hernández lunged to his left. The ball bounced near Jones's feet and past Hernández's shoulder, and Maddux loped to second base. The ball hit the backstop. Hernández chased it. And I stood near the front of the mound and watched all of it happen, sort of curious.

There'd actually been a pitch before that. Something weird. A fastball that didn't sit quite right. A fastball I'd wanted to throw inside to a right-handed hitter. And, well, here's the thing about me throwing a fastball inside to right-handers—I didn't want to leave it over the plate and anywhere near a bat barrel. In meant in. So, and it seemed subconscious, almost defensive, I'd let my wrist turn ever so slightly, and my fingers would fall to the left side of the ball, and that would change the rotation of the ball and therefore its path, and that pitch, just about every time, would run a few inches toward the hitter right at the end. It got a lot of strikeouts in there. It broke a few bats. Matheny knew about this because he had seen it hundreds of times. The ball was going to run that way. In a play-off game on national television by a rookie with a six-run lead? Maybe an inch or two more than usual. So I threw that, and it beat Hernández on the glove side, flat beat him, and skipped to the backstop, and I'd been wondering about that pitch, hanging on it emotionally maybe a little longer than usual. It didn't register anywhere else, just a ball, nobody on base, maybe a cross-up in signs, an unre-markable pitch at an unremarkable moment to which no one else gave another thought. Maybe it was trying to tell me what was coming, the only warning I'd get, and maybe it was nothing until I made it into something, until the curveball, and the groan from the crowd, and the game beginning to shift, and when I wanted to throw a fast-ball would I get that fastball again, the impertinent one? I waited for a new ball, held up my glove, waited to get back at it.

Huh, I thought. *I just threw a wild pitch.*

My mom was in the stands that afternoon. My father wasn't; he was serving a six-year federal prison sentence for conspiracy to possess with intent to distribute cocaine and marijuana. He'd lightened the sentence by rolling over on the guy who ran the smuggling ring—his boss, basically—which sounded about like my father. His term had begun a few months early because sometime between being sentenced and actually reporting for the sentence, he'd been picked up for carrying a pistol. Well, for flinging that pistol out of a window of a car the police were following, shortly after he'd brandished that pistol at a fellow traveler. This sort of development might have unhinged a normal family. For us, the hinge had always been squeaky. We'd learned to live with it, ignored it, figured a colicky hinge was better than no hinge at all. Besides, sometimes the authorities would come fix it, at least temporarily.

Though I was named for my grandfather, Richard Leo Turton, irony held that the name was close to that of Richard Patrick Ankiel, my father. For that distinction, I'd paid with parts of my childhood. I didn't hate him then. Not always. I wanted him to love me, and love my mom, and act like it. The hate would come later.

When anyone asked, my father was a professional drywaller. Or he was a professional fishing guide. Sometimes he really was too. According to the local cops, however, he was a professional drug smuggler, a thief, a habitual crook who'd been collared at least a couple dozen times and convicted half that, sometimes with my half-brother alongside.

You can't pick your father. You're assigned a father. And if you're lucky, he's not the guy in the aluminum stands calling your pitches and screaming at your coach, and he's not the guy on the barstool while you're asleep in the backseat of the car in the parking lot on a school night, and he's not the guy whose business brings the DEA to the front door during breakfast, and he's not the guy who abuses your mother in drunken fits. I was not lucky.

The upshot to his being a two-bit crook and not some criminal mastermind was that he got caught a lot, and then it didn't take long before he'd done his time and was home again and in a very foul mood.

He was my father. But nowhere did it say I had to be his son, not forever. I took the calls from prison and tried to explain to him that, yes, I was healthy, and, no, I didn't know what had happened, and, yes, maybe it was mechanical, and, no, he could not just fix this, certainly not from a prison pay phone in the Florida panhandle, and, yes, OK, I'd send along some autographs for his new friends on the cell block. There were enough voices inside my head already, voices of doubt and fear and approaching panic. There wasn't room for another. I'd already done that time.

If it was unfair that I'd fought my way out of that house and out from under my father for all those years only to step into an arena where there could be no winner, then it didn't occur to me at the time. If, by grinding my self-esteem semibare, he'd contributed to that single pitch and the emotional pandemonium it wrought, I'd refuse to recognize such weakness. This was me. All me. The ball in my hand, a strike to throw, and a game to win. That's it. They could whisper all they wanted about my "background," my "upbringing," all that nonsense, like it had caught up to me at the worst time, when a week before it had been my background and upbringing that had made me a competitor, a fighter, the man who would take a game one start at twenty-one years old and not flinch.

Until, like my left arm had grazed the third rail, I flinched.

I exhaled, composed myself, decided to move on, and threw another pitch to the backstop. Then a walk. Another wild pitch. A wild pitch for a walk. Another wild pitch. *Uh-oh*, I thought. *This isn't going away*, I thought. Braves kept coming to the plate, and I kept coming undone. Spiked curveballs, fastballs to the screen, poor Carlos Hernández, sore back and all, looking like a hockey goalie defending the world's largest net, the crowd not sure whether it should be boisterous in its support or solemn in its discomfort. I was going to pieces out there, and my breath was leaving in gasps, in part because of the anxiety and in part because I was racing to cover the plate every other pitch. Brian Jordan, the Braves' number-five hitter, singled, and I could have hugged him for swinging at the first pitch. (At a Cardinals fantasy camp sixteen years later, I did hug Brian, and we laughed when I told him the reason.) I was over thirty pitches in the inning, and I hadn't had the slightest idea where most of them were heading when I let them go. The Braves had put one ball in play, and I'd allowed two runs. Then Walt Weiss singled and put me out of my misery. La Russa walked to the mound and waved in a reliever, and I handed the ball to La Russa. It was the first time in my life I was glad to leave a baseball field. I'd get used to it.

The tally for the third inning: thirty-five pitches, two hits, two runs, four walks, five wild pitches, and, it turned out, one psyche forever hobbled.

You know how many wild pitches Greg Maddux, the Braves' pitcher that day, threw that season? In 249 1/3 innings? One. Knowing him and his reputation for control and tactics, he probably did it on purpose too. You know how many years it had been since someone had thrown five in a single inning? A hundred and ten. You know what the record was for wild pitches in a postseason career? A whole career? Six. I was one away, and it had taken me all of twenty pitches from the first wild pitch to, as of that afternoon, the last.

I didn't remember much about it. Not the next day. Not a decade after. A lot of it looked the same after that. I didn't want to remember it. Nearly fifteen years later, I'd look at a video and be surprised at how together I appeared. Because I wasn't. I sat in the dugout and looked out at the mess I'd made and didn't say anything, didn't throw anything, didn't destroy anything, didn't feel like crying, didn't feel like anything. I was in shock, probably, the kind of shock that comes when a twenty-one-year-old learns he is vulnerable. There's a blind spot. There's something in there, deep in there, that's not right. And he's going to have to live with this for a while. Those boxers who get knocked out for the first time, they all bear the emptiness in their eyes. Presumably, 90 percent of it is from getting hit in the face so hard. But that other 10 percent? That's their invincibility leaking out. I may as well have been hit in the face and dragged to the bench. At least then I'd have had a bruise to show for it. An explanation.

I told everyone afterward that my delivery was out of whack, and this sort of thing would never happen again, and—ha ha—at least I'd put my name in the record book, but the truth was it would happen forever now, and I hadn't even gotten started on the record book, and my pitching career was officially and forever hopeless. That's a lot to digest after fifteen minutes of clumsiness and emotional free fall.

This thing, or "the monster," as my agent, Scott Boras, called it (though never in front of me), had trailed me—hounded me—like it had the rest, and it won. It undid me like it had pitchers Steve Blass and Mark Wohlers. Steve Sax and Chuck Knoblauch, second basemen, had it. So did Mackey Sasser and Gary Bennett Jr., catchers. Many more. Some were big leaguers. Most were guys no one had ever heard of. They'd lost their release point and then their nerve. Or maybe it was the other way around. Who's to say? It was the easy throws, and the men hired to make them, that were primarily afflicted. Sixty feet, six inches from the pitcher's rubber to the plate, another couple feet to the catcher's mitt. That same distance for the catchers. A little more for second basemen.

Oh, there were others. I heard plenty of their stories. The names would change, but they could all throw one day but not the next and never again, not like they once had. Their arms had vertigo, and it was, almost certainly, fatal. That was their story, from beginning to end. I didn't much care. Sure, I had some sympathy for them. A little. Soon I'd have empathy for them. But I had enough with just myself to deal with, and the stories of how they'd suffered and then failed didn't leave me much to ponder. What was there to learn from a guy who was skilled one day, unskilled the next, and out of baseball the day after that?

What I had instead were nightmares. Sometimes the perspective would change: I was watching myself pitch, or I was seeing a game through my own eyes. Either way, the ball was in my left hand, the batter waiting, the catcher raising his mitt. It was my job to throw it there. But it was more than a job. In my dream, taking that baseball and delivering it to that mitt was all I'd ever wanted. My life hung on that pitch. I hesitated. For, as simple as it seemed, I sensed disaster. The ball was too heavy. The air was too thick. I was sweating. Breathing too hard. What was I afraid of? People were watching, gaping, wondering why I wasn't doing anything, and I wanted to throw that ball, wanted desperately to, if only I could take another minute.

Give me time. A little more time.

I couldn't see the tunnel. Where was the tunnel? Finally, I'd nod and raise my right knee and tilt my head back and stride toward the plate and pull the ball from my glove. I'd pick up the catcher's mitt in the corner of my right eye, my arm would start back, and I'd push hard off my left leg and land on my right foot, my mechanics were perfect, feeling the slope of the mound, and this was going to happen. My arm would whip forward and I was going to throw a strike and then I'd throw another and then another. Forever. I'd be free again. Me again.

The ball would refuse to come out of my hand. My hand would refuse to release it. I would stumble forward, dragged by the momentum of the windup and gravity and the dreams of a thousand nights, horrified that the ball and I had remained attached to each other. I'd avert my gaze from the ball in my hand and find the people staring, judging, demanding to know what had happened. Disgusted by me. *Just throw the ball*, they'd say. *Just throw it. How freakin' hard could it be?*

I'd lie awake in the dead of night, waiting for my heart to settle, cursing this thing that would not leave me alone, not even in my sleep.

Man, could I have used a full night's sleep. Just some peace. I wanted them to please look away. Just look away.

I tried to drink those nights away. Medicate them away. I tried to pitch them away in the minor leagues, achingly far from the place I wanted to be and the pitcher I wanted to be, for the better part of four years. Then, when none of it worked, I walked away. There's a story there too, after I'd worn out my arm and head and patience for long enough, after I'd started over and discovered it would never be the same, and after I'd seen defeat in everyone else's eyes too.

So, yeah, eventually I walked away. But I wasn't done. I was starting over.

CHAPTER THREE

Denise Turton met this guy, Richard, in the summer of 1977. He was local, a surfer and a partier, good for a drink and a laugh.

She was new to Fort Pierce, Florida, twenty years old and single. She had a young son, Phillip. They'd taken a Greyhound bus from Buffalo, New York. She'd never seen the ocean. It took her breath away, as if she'd come all that way to find exactly where she belonged. This was home. She'd be happy here, and Phillip would too. She just knew it.

Her father—also named Richard—was worried. It could be a hard world out there, and his only daughter had this habit of trying to soften it a person at a time, and maybe that worked OK in their little neighborhood, in their little city, but what lay beyond those boundaries was a different matter, a different kind of hard.

Like his father before him and then his son, Richard Turton worked at the local automobile plant in Buffalo. He was a machinist. He enlisted in the army, served in World War II, and came home to be a machinist again. He was kind and gentle, with these unusual eyes—not brown, not hazel, but almost golden, with blue rings on the perimeter—and he never had to look twice to correct Denise's behavior or that of her older brother, Gary. Richard's wife, Denise's mom, was Mildred. She got the kids off to school and kept the house running and tended to Richard, who'd be weary at the end of the day. There was no tension. There was no shouting. They adored each other. They were perfect, as far as Denise was concerned.

By the time Denise reached middle school, however, Mildred was nearly incapacitated by back pain, something in her spine, the doctors said. Countless surgeries only seemed to worsen her condition, so she spent months bedridden, sometimes at home, more often in a hospital. Richard went to the hospital every night after work. He sat by her bed and held her hand and caught her up on the day and on the children, just as he would if she were at home, just as she had when she was happy and healthy and Richard would come home from work. Mildred died of what the doctors called "complications" from the last of her surgeries—maybe it was an infection, or maybe Mildred, at fifty-one, simply could fight no more. That was in 1976. Denise, barely twenty, was struck then by an urge to discover, to lift herself from the loss of a mother who'd been drifting away for nearly a decade.

Denise and Phillip left for Florida. Denise's friend Maureen had a daughter about Phillip's age, and the four of them traveled together. Maureen had relatives in Fort Pierce, a fishing, citrus, and cattle town on Florida's east coast two hours short of Miami. They stopped there, and Denise got a job waiting tables. The two young mothers and their children settled into a two-bedroom apartment that wasn't bad. Denise bought a little Datsun for $500 and then learned to drive it to the local community college, where she had signed up for accounting classes.

Little by little, she fell in with the locals near her age, mostly at the beach. Denise loved the beach. That's where she made her friends, and some of them were still her friends thirty-five years later. It's also where she met Richard, who, in thirty-five years, would not be. He would be the father of her second son, though.

When Richard Ankiel was about two years old, the Ankiels—Richard was the fourth of five children—moved from Syracuse, New York, to Fort Pierce. All but Richard's father. Richard's mother was on her own, surrounded by children and struggling to keep them clothed and fed. Richard was reluctant to talk about his childhood beyond vague references to his mother and alcohol and the sometimes violent boyfriends who came and went and how he and his brothers and sisters would scatter until things settled down. Then, at the end of those stories, Richard would shrug and wave it away, like it wasn't important anymore and couldn't touch him. "Whatever," he'd say.

Denise, though, came from a good home. She could show him the beauty in that. The ease and the peacefulness that comes with trust, and with the common goal of raising their two boys—Richard had taken to young Phillip and Phillip to Richard—and all in this delightful town of friendly people and perfect beaches. Richard wasn't so sure. He had his own life to live, which included another family—his ex-wife and their daughter—across town. He drank. He left. He grew jealous. He returned unhappy and looking to set things straight.

Denise, my mom, wished she'd had the sense to leave Richard. Right then. The bruises generally healed while my father was away.

My mother lives with me today in Jupiter. It's my wife, Lory, and I, our two boys, and Mom. Occasionally, but not lately, Phil. We have a rule: no talk about Dad. Otherwise, Mom gets sad about that part of her life and I get mad for her—and for me—and the conversation always leads us into the same dingy corner. It happened. It's gone. We wasted enough time on it when it was actually going on. He doesn't get to put us into that corner anymore, not with regrets or horrible memories or even a rueful laugh over how absurd it could be.

Truth is, I was a daddy's boy when I was very young. I wanted to please him. I wanted him to like being with us. I wondered why he was so mad, why the beer made him so mad. And Mom believed that somehow she could salvage what had become of our lives and make a family. She also couldn't bear to see me disappointed.

He lived with us sometimes. When he didn't, he would sometimes come visit. Or he'd call and ask if we—Phil and I—wanted to go fishing the next day or maybe go surfing. We'd say yes and hardly sleep the night before, because Dad was fun and made us laugh. It was comforting to have a father like the other kids, even if it was part-time.

We'd wake up early the next morning and get dressed and sit in the living room waiting for Dad's car to pull into the driveway at 9 o'clock, just like he said. At 10 one of us would turn on the TV, but not too loud, so we could hear the car. At 11 Mom would say that maybe we should go out and play, but we wouldn't, because Dad was coming and we wanted to go fishing or maybe surfing. By noon or 1 she'd tell us Dad had called and said he had to work instead, and that he'd said to tell us he was really sorry and would make it up to us, except the phone hadn't rung and we knew she was lying for him. The next Saturday, though, we'd be sitting on the couch at 9 o'clock again, wearing our stuff to go surfing, slathered in sunblock, smelling like coconuts, waiting on the sound of the car, trying not to cry.

The cruelest part was how good he could be to us when he had the time and nothing better to do. We'd get in the backseat with a whole day ahead, Dad in a great mood, surfboard strapped to the roof, waves rolling to the beach.

He'd turn up the radio, some country song playing, and we'd know what was coming.

"All right," he'd say, "we don't go anywhere until you guys start singing."

Didn't even matter if we'd never heard the song before.

We'd mumble into the refrain as soon as it was recognizable, grinning like this was the most embarrassing thing ever.

"Can't hear you," he'd say, and we'd ramp it up so the neighbors could hear, and he'd put the car in gear. Off we'd go, happy as we'd ever be, singing about honky-tonk bars and broken hearts. They were playing our song.

By the time I was nine or ten years old, Mom had run out of excuses for him, but she never stopped trying. She never stopped saying how sorry she was. She never stopped covering for him, because a boy needs a father, and a boy doesn't always need to know the whole truth of it. A little bit of a father was better than none, she believed, and if he could only see our faces when he drove up that driveway, or see them when he didn't, maybe he'd understand.

She'd do it all on her own if she had to. Her father, Richard, sent $200 so the electricity wouldn't be shut off. Or $100 to cover Little League fees and equipment. He sent Phillip and me cards with $20 bills tucked inside, always with the same handwritten note: "Don't spend it all in one place." She'd clip coupons and borrow rent money from friends and make do on a salary unfit for three if that's what the day brought. It was what every day brought.

She aimed for normal. Her only hope for that was for Dad to stay away. Then we'd find our routines. She'd go to work and we'd go to school. I'd come home, change out of my school clothes, make sure the kitchen wasn't a complete disaster, and be home by dinner. It was simple, just the three of us.

He'd find another girlfriend and be gone for months. He'd come back and apologize. Mom would think of us in the next room, or look into our faces, and then there'd be four of us again. She couldn't shake the notion that a boy should have a father nearby. She couldn't not believe in having a family, even if it were all fouled up and volatile and hurtful. The truth was, sometimes she mourned his absence, for the loneliness that came with it. Dad always had a warm place and a meal when his luck ran out everywhere else, and maybe that was the problem. Of course it was the problem.

Another problem was that Dad was a bully, and Mom, because she so wanted to believe the nightmare would end and didn't want to be threatened again and also didn't want to lie in a puddle of her own blood on the kitchen floor, was afraid. She had nowhere to go. She had two boys to raise and protect. She had to be brave. So she prayed the car she heard turn into the driveway wasn't his.

CHAPTER
FOUR

My father could be a decent, reasonable man. He taught me where the snook were. He put me on his shoulders when he surfed, or out on the front of the board, and we'd laugh all the way to shore. He hit me a lot of baseballs in the backyard.

Life could be OK, you know, from a distance.

Then he'd come home from Little Jim's, the bait shop and beer joint out on the causeway that would stay open until he was done, and in the time in between I'd gone from "son"—he almost always called me "son"—to "you fat fuck," and I wasn't close to getting the worst of it.

I was just a boy, and what could I do? Mom would scream, "Help! Help me!" and I would shiver from behind my bed. I would hear the kitchen drawer open and the blade of a knife slide across the others as it was drawn into the open, and I would hope she had armed herself against the monster in the kitchen. But she would scream again, and I would close my eyes and wish it would end, that he would go away forever, that we could be happy and normal like other families.

I would awaken in the morning like that, curled and hidden behind the bed, and for a few moments, while my eyes focused and the world came back into view, I wouldn't remember the rage and the threats and the wailing. I felt warm. I felt safe. I was just a boy, after all, and I could convince myself we'd be safe.

She stayed, though. We stayed. And he kept coming around when he felt like it. They never married, and he never acted as though they were, which explained the half-sister—the whole other family—across town. My mother couldn't leave because she was sure he would find her—find us—and kill her for running, because she was afraid he was always a beer or two from beating her or worse. So we stayed, and he drank, and on the nights when he did come home from Little Jim's—some of them with me behind the wheel, at twelve years old, because he kept running the car into trees—we would hope he was only desperately mean and not homicidal.

There would be some relief when the DEA agents came. They'd usually pull into the driveway before school, one car followed by a handful of others, their blue and red lights whirling across the house and the trees and the lawn and the neighbors' houses in the dawn's gray. By the time the agents knocked on the door and roused my father and explained there was a warrant—it was always drugs, marijuana or coke, smuggling or selling or holding or an old warrant or all of it—the folks next door and the people across the street and the family in the house next to theirs would be watching from behind curtains pulled clear of the front windows.

Then, while I sat at the kitchen table and finished my cereal and thought about the huge bag of marijuana I'd found stuffed behind the VCR, the agents would lead my father out of the house, parade him across the lawn, and ease him into the backseat of one of those cars. He'd be back. But not that day. I'd put my bowl in the sink, brush my teeth, kiss Mom on the cheek, and go to school, like it had all been part of the routine.

My mother—relieved, humiliated, spent—would stand in the corner of the kitchen, out of the way and, for a few hours, safe.

When the cars had pulled away one morning and the neighbors had left their windows, I told her, "I never want to be like that."

"You won't, Ricky," she said. "You won't."

She once gathered the courage to try life as a regular, single mother of two. It wasn't long after one of those mornings when the police came by to drag my belligerent father away, events my mother would call "Jerry Springer auditions," when the neighbors would come out from behind their curtains and onto their porches to witness the latest episode. She'd be too embarrassed to leave the house for an hour or two, but that would fade into the past embarrassments, and eventually, she'd have to go to work or the supermarket or the bank, so she'd put on her sunglasses and drive off. She didn't want to be that lady in that house, the loud house that disrupted everything. She hoped they understood that. Still, she avoided eye contact, as much for them as for her. It was awful and it was dangerous and she was sorry for that, but she hadn't found a way out.

She went on a date during a time when Dad was not around. I might've been five. Mom hired a babysitter, a big expense, and a man she knew took her for dinner and a movie. They returned to the house after a few hours at about 9:30, laughing and happy to have had an evening out.

Dad was waiting in the bushes. He ordered Mom into the house and beat the hell out of the guy. She watched from inside, screaming at Richard to stop or she'd call the cops. She did not call the cops. She never called the cops, because eventually they'd leave and she'd be alone and Dad would punish her for it, she just knew it. She waited for the beating to end, then watched her date open the door of his car, get behind the wheel, and drive off. He was headed to the emergency room, where they'd stitch his face up.

My old man was an asshole. I didn't want him to be. I'd like to think he didn't want to be. But there we were. Whatever.

He chose. Every day, it seemed, he chose. So the games of catch in the backyard were washed away in those choices, and so were those mornings hunting snook, those afternoons on the surfboard, those evenings watching the Braves games, when he'd take me out back under the dim lights and just for kicks teach me to throw a knuckleball, when I thought he was the coolest thing to ever be, that ever walked in. Which he did sometimes, just walked in like it was all OK. And the way he walked, all proud and full of himself, made a boy like me believe it must be true. That I had to be wrong about him.

My mom must've done something to piss him off. I must be a disappointment. The cops must have it in for him. Phil, my brother, who had protected me with his fists more than once, must like the work and be good at it, and Dad wouldn't ever let him get into trouble. No dad does that, right? So we all went along. For a long time, we went along. I worshipped him and asked myself not to be too disappointed. And I grew harder. And I asked people to like me. Not out of duty or because of a street address or because of my name or because I could throw a ball. Because of me. The alternative was more disappointment. More violence. The alternative was watching Phil go off to jail too, because of the drugs, because of where that started, selling them and using them with the man who should've helped raise him and instead made him an accomplice. I was too small, and then I was too afraid, and even when I grew up there remained the notion that to challenge one's father was to call out the whole universe into the middle of the street to decide who was the better man. And how long would that have lasted? A punch or two? And what would that have cost my mother in bruises?

He'd have beaten the shit out of me, and nothing would change. Or I'd have caught him with fists and anger and youth, and he'd laugh and be back tomorrow. So I kept my mouth shut, and usually I forgave myself for it. I wished for peace for my mother. I'd lie in bed and close my eyes as tight as I could and wait for the shouting, the screaming, the cries for help to pass. When he left I hoped it was forever, and I knew better. A day later we'd be in the backyard, me and the guy who had terrorized my mother and left her crying again, lobbing a baseball back and forth, talking about the Braves' rotation, trying those knuckleballs on each other, laughing when the ball would wobble and sail. *We're safe*, I'd whisper. *Mom's safe too. It's going to be all right. It's going to change.*

My old man was an asshole, though, and by the time I figured that out, was old enough to know, he'd already wrecked two of us. That left me. I can't exactly say where that left me. But I knew I wasn't wrecked. I wouldn't give him the satisfaction.

He'd have to be a hell of a lot meaner, I told myself. *He'd have to be drunker. And now that I'm old enough and big enough, he can't beat me. Because I don't care. That's where I win. Because I won't even fucking care.* You can't beat a man who doesn't fucking care.

Maybe he hated his life and hated us for it. I don't know. I found a better father, anyway, along the way, in a man named Harvey. And then I found a better father in me. It shouldn't have had to go that way. It did. Over and over. Whatever, man. Whatever. I'd find my own way, and he wasn't invited.

CHAPTER
FIVE

When I was thirteen, my best friend died. His name was Dennis. He lived a couple blocks over in a single-story house that was small and rectangular, nothing special, really, like a lot of the houses in Fort Pierce. I loved it there, because Dennis was there, and because it wasn't my house, which was structurally fine but could be emotionally unsteady.

There Dennis and I played one-on-one games of whatever sport was in season, but mostly we played baseball. Our game was simple: I pitched, he hit, and I tried to catch it. Then we switched. The corner of the house, a dirt path, the neighbor's house, and the telephone line marked the singles, doubles, triples, and home runs, in our imaginations the very dimensions of Atlanta–Fulton

County Stadium, where the great Dale Murphy played. We chased foul balls into the woods that ran up against his backyard, and sometimes we'd get distracted by something in the woods and not come back until after dinnertime. Even by the shallow measures of good and bad at the age of thirteen, I knew Dennis was good, and I knew we were safe. There was plenty in Fort Pierce that wasn't, some of it just a couple blocks over.

Sometimes Dennis came to my house, which was fine too, because my father was everybody else's best friend. Pretty much, you liked my dad and my dad liked you, as long as you weren't me. Or my mother. But then, eventually, Dennis would have to go home.

Dennis lived with his mother and little brother. His father lived in Boca Raton. I met him once. That was at the funeral. I was a pallbearer.

We didn't do much without each other. Dennis was left-handed like me, and we both always hit the ball to the right side. So we didn't need a left field, and those sorts of conveniences seemed important at the time. In my backyard, the trees were over there anyway. He played the outfield and pitched, like me.

We spent the night wherever the day ran out, his house or mine, it didn't matter as long as the coast was clear, and if I wasn't home by dark, my mom knew I was at Dennis's, trying to hit a near invisible tennis ball as far as I could against my best friend. We'd talk about playing for the Atlanta Braves, alongside Sid Bream and David Justice and John Smoltz and Tom Glavine, and we'd imagine what it would be like to win the lottery and have that life instead.

By then, Dennis and I had been like this for going on half our lives—brothers by all but blood. I hated to see him go. Man, he should've seen me in my Braves uniform when I was grown up. He would have loved that.

My mom and dad and I went away one weekend. I was playing in a baseball tournament in Sarasota, which was kind of a big deal, because it was all the way across the state and we'd stay in a hotel. Only, when it came time for the game, Mom wouldn't leave the room, and she seemed upset, and after the game, we picked her up at the hotel and drove three hours home in a very quiet car.

Once in the living room, having hauled in my duffel bag and two days of dust and sweat, I announced, "I'm going over to Dennis's." Something caught in my mom's throat. I was half out the door when she said, "Honey, wait a minute. You can't go." She handed me a newspaper clipping. There'd been an accident, it said. A bunch of kids were in a car, and it crashed, and Dennis was in the front passenger seat. His name was in the paper. He'd died in that car while I was off playing baseball.

In that moment, I swore that nothing would ever hurt me that badly again. It was bigger than the sadness I felt. The loss I felt. The anger that bit my cheeks. It was bigger than all the friends I would ever make again and the people standing in the living room with me. If that car was going to flip over and take Dennis, then it would take parts of me too, and I didn't care. That's how I wanted it, and that's how I would keep it.

I went to Dennis's house anyway. I stood in the street and didn't knock on the door or go in. In some ways, it was my home too, and that was my family in there, and I cried for what they'd lost and I'd lost. I cried for what we'd lost. Us, together. But I didn't go in.

In the weeks, maybe months, that followed, I'd walk the couple blocks, stand in the road, and stare at his front door. I didn't want to believe it, I guess. I wanted him to walk out the door, nod, and say, "Hey, Ricky," like it had never happened, and then I could pretend it had never happened, and we could go back to dreaming again, and we would be safe again.

I thought a lot about being safe then.

CHAPTER
SIX

In my teens I could pretty well distinguish between right and wrong. Wrong, you see, stumbled into the house plenty of nights. Wrong dragged my older brother, Phillip, along with it to run drugs. Wrong got hauled off in handcuffs, sometimes with Phillip, wearing a matching set, a few steps behind.

Right killed the summer nights playing ball in the Florida heat. Right maybe sneaked a beer or two from somebody's dad's supply, but it never did any harm.

On the night before an Independence Day in Fort Pierce, five of us drove over to White City Park. I was thirteen, hanging out with some older kids. Our honest intention was to play a game we'd dreamed up long ago on one of these same boring nights, not much else going on in a sleepy beach town for young men who sort of knew right from wrong.

We had a Wiffle Ball and bat. The rules were loose. The game usually was fun enough for a few hours anyway. We played on the tennis courts, and on that night we pulled open the fence door, laughing and dogging each other on who was gonna take who deep. We fed a quarter into the slot over the knob that would turn on the lights. No lights. Another quarter. Nothing. We shook the coin box and wrestled the knob and listened to our lonely quarters rattle. We looked at each other.

And, well, it's funny how the smallest of inconveniences can become the biggest of messes. How, exactly, I ended that night sprawled in a police-station parking lot, my hands bound behind my back, my father standing over me, was a lesson in dumbness and idle minds. While it was indeed my father who accounted for my skidding, knee-scraping, concrete landing, that accounting for the final few feet of a poorly conceived evening, it was one of our few father-son moments in which I looked up at his glowering face and granted, "Yeah, I probably had that coming."

Of course there was some hypocrisy in his being mad at me for running up against the law. Maybe he had a moment of clarity, of regret for the example he was setting for his son on the streets and waterways around Fort Pierce. Maybe he was pissed because he'd had to leave the bar to come sign for me.

Anyway, by the time he reached into the backseat of the patrol car and chucked me onto the pavement, I was far less concerned with what the cops and courts were about to do to me than I was with what my dad had in mind.

"Sir," one of the policemen said to my father. I recall being surprised he didn't know my father's name. "You're going to have to wait until we're done with him."

My father looked at me and growled, "You better hope they keep your ass."

Which was not particularly comforting.

No, I was going to pay for the previous couple hours, and I was going to remember them for a long time, and I wasn't ever going to find myself on the wrong side of the patrol car's cage again if I could help it.

Sitting in the darkness at White City Park, one of the guys had gotten to talking about this car he wanted to buy, which made little sense because he didn't have any money, but a young man can dream. We decided this car he couldn't afford was going to need a stereo and some other accessories, which of course he couldn't afford either, which was what led us to a couple car dealerships and parking lots in town. By the time we were done that night, the trunk of our car was loaded with stereos and speakers. As I recall, a half-dozen squad cars stopped us as we were leaving the bowling alley, the scene of our final caper. I knew they'd find the sound equipment, and so did they.

I considered running. In fact, we were apprehended along the route I would run home from dinner, so I knew I could cover it with ease. But there were so many of them. Their lights were everywhere. People were slowing down to witness the spectacle. And the cops looked serious. My heart hit my stomach. Damn, I didn't want to be involved in this. *That's not me*, I thought. *That's* him.

Two of us in the back of one police car and two in the back of another, off we went, and when our car stopped at a gas station, my buddy leaned forward and asked, "What, we stoppin' for donuts?"

The policeman turned around.

"Laugh it up," he said. "Some big ol' guy named Bubba's gonna be waiting for you. Gonna change your name to Sweet Cheeks."

Oh, my God, I thought. *Oh, my God*. I didn't want to be anybody's Sweet Cheeks, and certainly not Bubba's.

We left the gas station (no donuts for us), and when we arrived at the police station, my father pulled in behind us. He half walked, half ran to the open door, reached in, and grabbed a couple fistfuls of my shirt, my arms pinned behind my back.

I spent the night in a holding cell. Never did meet Bubba. There'd be court hearings, probation, restitution. I wrote letters to the owners of the car lots, apologizing for my deeds. Before that, I came out of jail, squinting through the midmorning light to my waiting parents. I half didn't want to go.

"Don't ever fuck up again," my father said and cuffed my head.

Even then, at thirteen, with almost zero perspective on a world beyond a sidewalk outside a police station in a little Florida beach town where the locals really should've locked up their stereos, I couldn't help but think, *Ain't that rich.*

CHAPTER
SEVEN

I saw the catcher's mitt. I heard nothing. Early on, I heard my father droning from the bleachers or railing from the backstop. Now I heard nothing. I felt the ball in my hand.

Thinking, but not really thinking, *I'm going to put the ball right there.*

When it was right, I was in touch with everything. A nick on the surface of the ball under my thumb. A dangling lace from the catcher's mitt. A gob of mud under my left spike, under the foot from which I'd drive from the rubber.

As if I weren't playing the game exactly but was part of the game itself. I was the heartbeat, the pulse that kept everything else moving, the game flowing all around and through me. And I was the part that was going to take that baseball and blow it by hitters who thought they knew better. I had the fastball to do it. I had the beginnings of the curveball. I had this knuckleball I thought was pretty clever. I had the resolve.

Always had, really. From the time I was old enough to recognize the difference between a good ballplayer and a better one, I knew in my heart I was the latter. I was small, probably too small at first, but I didn't care.

It's why I would pull my shoulders back the way I did and walk with the confidence I did. It's why my eyes, my grandfather's eyes, would sear a hole straight through a batter's chest, and I would harden that with a casualness; the way I held the ball loose in my hand, the way I set my feet softly over the rubber, the way I'd soar into my windup and finish it with a look that said, *That's the way it was supposed to end.*

It started in my backyard and on the dirt tracks of Fort Pierce. It started in Port St. Lucie Little League and over at Sportsman's Park on Prima Vista Boulevard. It started at Port St. Lucie High School, home of the Jaguars, under head coach John Messina, class of '97, where I was *USA Today*'s national player of the year, where I was 11–1 with an 0.47 ERA and struck out 162 batters in 74 innings (of the 222 outs I registered that senior season, 60 did not come by strikeout), where nobody ever hit more home runs, where the last swing of my career launched a 420-foot home run, where no one will ever again wear the number 24, and where a coach once said, "I don't think I'll ever see another one like him." It was where Coach Messina taught me how to be a ballplayer, or as much as one could be as a teenager. It started with my turning down a scholarship offer from the University of Miami to sign with the St. Louis Cardinals for $2.5 million, and then with my becoming Baseball America's eighteenth-best prospect after the 1997 season, second-best prospect after the 1998 season, and top prospect after the 1999 season.

When I was in high school and a magazine reported that I was on the chubby side for a top-end prospect, I ran. When my family went for dinner at the local burger joint, I'd have my share and then refuse the ride home. I'd run those miles, some of them along a narrow thoroughfare in Fort Pierce called, innocently and in spite of the evidence to the contrary, Easy Street. Over the winter, outside baseball season, when the coaches were seeding the rye grass so the Bermuda wouldn't go dormant and then spending hours on the field with water hoses to keep it alive, I'd run the bleachers. I could be a clumsy kid. I was shy. Life at home was difficult, and sometimes a lot worse. On a baseball field I was more refined. I was sure. I was safe. Try as they might, nobody could hurt me there. That was where I did the hurting. And I really loved the game, particularly as I grew and my body became strong, when I wasn't the smallest anymore. It felt wonderful to belong to something that loved me back. Baseball wasn't moody. When we won or lost, when I was good or bad, it was because the game was wholly rational. Out there, you deserved what you got, win or lose.

The improvement was nearly imperceptible to me, but my fastball was coming. I threw 80 mph, maybe a bit more if the wind was helping, as a sophomore at Port St. Lucie.

Early in my junior season, I was pushing 90 and could get 90 when I needed it, and by that June, 92 and 93 felt easy. An assistant coach, a nice man named Tony Malizia, became the pitching coach in 1997, my senior season, and so became the gatekeeper as far as scouts were concerned. He did a good job, because I hardly noticed them, beyond the fact that there'd be a bunch of old guys in Panama hats and loose flowery shirts hanging around games who'd never been around before. We'd get off the bus, and there they'd be, waiting. Watching. Deciding if I was their guy.

The outgoing message on his answering machine at school reported something along the lines of "You've reached Tony Malizia at Port St. Lucie High School. Rick Ankiel next pitches Friday afternoon at home. Otherwise, leave a message."

There were stories. The day I warmed up in the bull-pen, feeling my fastball, and broke the webbing on the catcher's mitt. He had another in his duffel bag. In the second inning, he called time and turned to the umpire. That mitt had broken too, and he was fresh out of mitts. The rest of the game, opposing catchers shared the same mitt. They'd leave it on home plate between innings.

I was good, and I was having fun. It was important to me to be good. Life otherwise could be wobbly at times. There was the afternoon I struck out the first nineteen batters in a seven-inning game. I hit the twentieth batter and then picked him off first base. The twenty-first bunted straight back to me. There was the afternoon I threw a no-hitter and the opposing pitcher threw a one-hitter. That was cool, as the one hit he allowed was my home run.

My last game, in the regional final, when a win would have sent us to the state playoffs, we lost. I pitched. We were behind by a few runs, and my pitch count was approaching ninety, and the draft was coming, and there was no reason for me to keep pitching. We were in Dunedin. The opposing crowd gave me a standing ovation, which was thrilling. I'd never been that guy before. And in my last at bat, I hit a ball over the center-field fence

It's not to say there wasn't always plenty of noise from the bleachers. My father, after all, was at a lot of my games.

He viewed himself, I came to believe, as my coach. I believed that because he said so a lot. And then, at practices and games, he'd talk over the men who were supposed to be my coaches. If he weren't close enough to talk over them, he'd yell. I'd try to ignore it and not be embarrassed by what I couldn't ignore, because that behavior was not going to change. The big personality, the life-of-the-party outside voice, the smartest-guy-in-the-room assurance, none of that went away because he was behind a chain-link fence. So I pitched. And I hit. And I looked straight ahead. And my coaches put up with it, and I did too.

When the yelling started at home, I'd push it out of my head. I'd close the door and find something else to think about. The next morning, the four of us—Dad, Mom, Phillip, and I—would fix breakfast and wash up and walk out the door as though the night before had not happened. Maybe it wasn't healthy, but it was better than taking a chance that a conversation would ignite more of the same. We were never going to sit in a circle and hold hands and tell each other how we felt. We were, however, going to pretend everything was fine and, when possible, avoid eye contact.

So, by the time I got to the mound or the batter's box, I was practiced in the art of self-preservation, of compartmentalization. I'd push it all out of my head and throw a strike, even if Dad were shouting at me to throw the knuckler. Though, granted, sometimes I did. There was a lot going on.

My senior year, we were playing Jacksonville Bolles at Port St. Lucie. I was pitching well. We were ahead by a few runs. In the bottom of the sixth inning, the pitching coach, Tony Malizia, came to me and said, "You're done." I nodded.

My pitch count wasn't too high. I felt fine. But the draft was coming, and Tony took care of me first and then the score. I appreciated that. I loved to play and loved to win and felt safe in his hands. He would not overwork my arm, which I was going to need for the next twenty years or so.

The bottom of the sixth was passing a little too fast, however. The guy who was supposed to relieve me wasn't ready. "Tell you what, Ricky," Tony said. "Go get the first out, and then I'll come get you." I nodded again. Whatever. I wanted to pitch.

I don't recall the particulars of what happened next. My father thought I should not pitch anymore. That I remember. There were eight players on the field to start the seventh inning, and I was not one of them, and there was no pitcher on the mound. That I sort of remember. Everyone was staring into the dugout.

"Ricky!" Tony said. "You're pitching!"

And I responded, "My dad doesn't want me out there."

At which point Tony turned to my dad, who was looking for trouble and went ballistic, shouting something about ruining my arm, and, well, by the time all that was done, the guy who was going to pitch the seventh was warm. Thank goodness for my mom, who'd sit quietly with the other moms and smile and thank my coaches no matter the final score. They adored her, and that was something, even when dear old Dad was reaming out the guy who was simply trying to do his best by me.

Most of that story I got from Tony years later. It made me wonder what else I'd pushed away, what else I'd conveniently forgotten and didn't want to know.

As Tony told it, the next morning he was in the press box at the baseball field preparing for practice. There was a knock on the door. When he opened it, my father and I were standing there. Dad apologized for the outburst and added that he knew Tony had my best interests at heart. They shook hands. And I went back to playing baseball. Down there. Beyond the chain-link fence.

Maybe by then, I was already gone. Gone from under the drama that was my mother and father. Gone from inside the house that kept it all closed up, airtight, so when the finger-drum of tension approached I could hardly breathe. Gone from the town that reminded me of where I would not—could not—end up. My mother didn't deserve the life she got, and I would not—could not—choose the same. I was going to chase something better. I was going to let myself dream and go after that.

CHAPTER
EIGHT

The 1997 draft was coming. I hired Scott Boras to advise me, with the intention of hiring him as an agent if that went well. Otherwise, I had a scholarship offer from the University of Miami and even signed a letter of intent, which I considered a good option in spite of the fact that I really didn't have much use for school. In high school I did just enough homework to get by and gutted my way through tests, sometimes by actually studying for them, other times by having friends who'd already taken the test and were kind enough to pass along the questions and/or answers. School was about survival. That may not sound like the best approach to take to college, but it didn't seem to bother the colleges. I'd originally been taken with Florida State, which rescinded its scholarship offer when it became clear I would have to choose the Seminoles over millions of dollars. They offered that scholarship to someone else. That meant Miami. On my recruiting trip, one of the administrators asked brightly, "Hey, is there anything you're worried about?"

"Yeah," I said. "My grades."

He grinned and winked and said, "Don't worry about it."

I said, "Where do I sign?"

I loved Miami already.

I wanted to play professional baseball. And Florida State was right—I wasn't walking away from instant wealth. Major-league teams probably knew this, so the Miami option didn't scare them off that much. They were probably more worried that I was working with Scott.

The year before, Matt White, a high school right-hander from Pennsylvania, Bobby Seay, a left-handed pitcher from Sarasota High School, and Travis Lee, a first baseman at San Diego State, were the Boras studs. The Minnesota Twins took Lee with the second pick, the San Francisco Giants took White with the seventh pick, and the Chicago White Sox took Seay with the twelfth. Well, Scott had discovered a loophole in the collective bargaining agreement, and the three were declared free agents. Lee signed with the Arizona Diamondbacks for $10 million. White got $10.2 million and Seay $3 million from the Tampa Bay Devil Rays. None would be even average big-league players. Because of injuries, White never threw a big-league pitch.

Teams and their scouts didn't know how any of the three of their careers would turn out in 1997, of course, but Boras's reputation suggested to them that the 17-year-old lefty in Port St. Lucie wasn't going to come cheap. I was sort of counting on that, as was my father. Because of our strategy and teams' general reluctance to spend on amateur talent, Scott told us we'd fall in the draft, even if several publications said I was the nation's top prospect. It didn't stop the scouts from coming around and clogging the parking lots and bleachers. I didn't pay them much mind, even when they followed teammates to the bathroom to ask, "Hey, what's Rick really like?," even when they'd drop a pen through the fence at the feet of a teammate and upon its return ask, "Hey, tell me about Rick. Know his dad?"

Everybody knew my dad.

Scott prepared us for the day of the draft. Teams were going to avoid me for as long as they could. We had the leverage of Miami. We had the leverage of my arm. It was Scott's job not to blink. He was very good at not blinking and told my father and me it could be a long day but it would end well, eventually. We'd get our money.

"We better," my father told him.

The New York Mets had the sixth pick. They'd been around a lot. I knew their scouts a little. I knew a lot of scouts a little. The Mets tried to negotiate a predraft deal and offered, I think, just under $2 million. They called me directly, hoping to outmaneuver Scott. I turned them down, on Scott's advice.

Fifty-two amateur players went in the first round. Finally, when that round was done, my phone rang. This was 1997, before I could have followed along in real time on a computer. I reached for the phone, thinking, *All right, I got drafted.*

"Hello?" I said, sounding respectful and curious about what my first professional team would be.

"How does it feel," a voice said, "to slip out of the first round?"

The line went dead.

I recognized the voice. It belonged to a Mets scout. I turned to my mother and father and said, "I ever see that guy, I'm gonna slap the shit out of him."

Never did see him.

So we waited in the living room and found other stuff to talk about and watched the clock. I didn't care where I went in the draft, but I was eager to get on with it. In the middle of the afternoon, the screen door opened, and a local newspaper reporter, a camera hanging from his neck, was standing in front of us. My mother smiled, sure this would all work out, and then amused by the stranger among us.

"Get the hell outta here," my father shouted and started toward the reporter, who beat it off the porch and across the yard with his own camera whipping him as he ran.

Dad might have been stressed by then. We didn't talk about it much, but it seemed that my being the first pick was important to him, and then the whole first round had come and gone, along with who knows how much money—he didn't fully trust Scott—and that reporter was fortunate we didn't live out the rest of the day putting him back together. I knew my talent. I assumed it was worth something. Scott was good at this.

The second round came, and the clock kept spinning, and my father got redder. He was pacing. I started to get the feeling he thought it wasn't just my money in jeopardy. It was his too. But we were getting along, and he was spending time at home, and my mom seemed happy, and there always seemed to be something about to set him off, and here we were in the second round. The fiftieth pick passed, then the sixtieth, then the seventieth.

The phone rang again. It was Scott. The Cardinals, he said. Seventy-second overall.

"Who are the Cardinals?" I said.

I wanted to be a Brave. I really only knew the Braves. They had the eightieth pick. I'd waited around that long. What would be another eight picks?

"Oh, man, that sucks," I said.

"No, no, no," Scott said. "It's a strong organization. It's a good thing. They're a good team. It's a really, really good thing."

It was June 2. I packed to pitch for a USA Baseball eighteen-and-under team that would include future big leaguers Matt Holliday, Michael Cuddyer, and Koyie Hill. Two and a half months later, I was in my room, packing to go to Miami. Maybe I was going to college after all.

Negotiations between Scott and the Cardinals were arduous, nearly three months running, though both seemed to know there would be agreement. In midsummer, Walt Jocketty, the Cardinals' general manager, came to Fort Pierce. He drove up to the house with a man I didn't know. I shook their hands, introduced them to my mom, and then crawled into the backseat of the car. We headed to Jupiter, where they showed me some dirt and grass that one day would be the Cardinals' spring training and minor league facility. They pointed and described where the buildings would be, then pointed in another direction, and that was where the stadium would be, and then reminded me how close I was to home and my parents.

They seemed nervous. I felt fine.

On the ride home, Walt asked me if I thought I was ready for pro ball. I smiled. Scott had told me he'd ask me that. The question was meant as a challenge, like I could step up and play with the big boys or go hide in college with the other seventeen-year-olds.

"I'm 100 percent ready," I said.

Walt nodded.

"But you have to convince my dad," I added. "He got me this far. So I'm going to trust what he says now."

Just like Scott had told me.

That was the play. Lay it on my father, who would be the bad guy. The richer I got, the richer he assumed he'd get. The summer went on like that. I went to play ball. The last game I pitched, in the days before the deadline to sign, I struck out sixteen or seventeen guys, scouts all over the stands. Scott assured me that the Cardinals would come around, that the money would be there. I gassed up the car and filled a suitcase for the two-hour drive to freshman orientation.

Were I to enter a Miami classroom, there'd be no money until I was draft eligible again, years away. I'd be a college man. I'd have to study and take tests, which, in spite of assurances that I'd be seen through any difficulties, was a little intimidating. I also trusted Scott, who'd convinced me I was worth more than most anyone who'd gone before me. So if I were going to have to sit in lecture halls and continue with the aluminum bats for a couple years, then I'd dutifully report to freshman English at the appointed time and maybe find someone to help with my homework.

Matt Anderson, the first pick in the draft, didn't sign with the Detroit Tigers until December 23. He was a college pitcher. J. D. Drew, another Scott client, was taken second by the Philadelphia Phillies, who offered $2.6 million. He did not sign; instead he played in an independent league, another loophole Scott had discovered. (The Cardinals got J. D. with the fifth pick in 1998. The signing bonus was $7 million.) Troy Glaus, the third pick, signed in late September. Jeff Weaver, a college pitcher and Scott client, went sixty-second, ten picks ahead of me, to the Chicago White Sox. He did not sign.

According to the rules of the draft, the moment I walked into one of those classrooms, I'd be ineligible to sign. That was the Cardinals' deadline. I was packing to go and willing to live with either outcome. Hey, college might be fun.

Before I left, I spent one last night with my friends at a house not far from mine. My pager lit up. The Cardinals had offered $2.1 million. Scott believed he could get them higher still, and by the next day the number was $2.5 million, the fifth-highest bonus ever paid. The only job I'd ever had was helping a friend's father tear up carpet and scrape floors. He'd pay me out of his pocket. I didn't have a checking account. I didn't have a savings account. Whatever money I had was in my wallet, maybe $50, but probably not.

And then I was rich. I was really rich. After taxes and fees, and after going to the bank, the number on the statement was something like $1,300,000. I went to the mall with my two best friends, strode into the record store, and said, "Whatever CDs you want."

I got twelve. Rap, country, pop. One techno. I bought my mom a car. She was grateful. She was happy for me.

Then there was Dad, who, it seemed, was happy for him.

He had plans. A condo the next town over. A building in Melbourne he'd renovate. A whole building for just $900 grand, he said. Houses on the river. If not the building, he said, then surely one of these $400,000 houses on the river. You know, for the family. For us. My father, suddenly the real estate magnate. The family man.

"I'm the reason you're so good," he said. "I got you here. You owe me."

I wrote him a check for, I think, $25,000. Called it a finder's fee. His cut for his part in putting me on Earth, for playing catch against a few evening suns, for being a pitching coach when he didn't have something better to do, for yelling at me when I was too small and not very good at fourteen years old, and for sitting out a few games of fall baseball. They say you can't put a price on that, on the relationship between a father and son, on the years a father spends turning his boy into a man and refraining from calling him "you fat fuck." I did and called us even. The stroke of a pen. Thanks for everything.

I rented a house, threw a couple suitcases in the back of the truck, told my mother I'd visit as often as I could, and went off—at eighteen—to become a professional baseball player.

CHAPTER
NINE

The Cardinals held their Instructional League in St. Petersburg, a three-hour drive west from Fort Pierce across Florida. I made the drive in the fall of 1997 and dragged my bags into an apartment I'd share with Bobby Seay and Matt White. You could have called it the house that Boras built.

Matt, the college guy who had $10 million in the bank, was often the adult in the room. He also left his wallet around occasionally, which was a mistake.

The days were filled with baseball, Matt and Bobby—they were Devil Rays—in one direction, me in the other. By early evening we'd return dusty and sunburned to the apartment, our heads clogged from learning new names and routines and mechanics. The first days could be confusing, but it was still baseball, and so it was fun, and the three of us would recount the early trials of learning to become big leaguers.

None of us was much of a cook, so we'd go for a steak or pasta and continue the conversation at a nearby restaurant. The meals were always on Matt, only he didn't know it. See, Bobby and I had lifted a credit card out of the wallet Matt left unguarded. When the restaurant bill arrived, we'd let Matt offer, then one of us would insist, "Nah, I got this," and pay with Matt's card. When Matt went to bed, the credit card was returned to his wallet. A few weeks later, Matt opened his credit-card statement. While he stood staring at the page, his forehead crinkled, Bobby and I thanked him for all the dinners. Slowly, very slowly, Matt broke into a grin.

"Jerks," he said, or something like it.

Therefore, I got what I probably had coming at camp. Karma and all. Some of the older guys saw me coming. We had to be in the clubhouse and in uniform for a meeting by 8 in the morning. A minute late brought a fine. My routine got me there—every day—at exactly 7:57. So, technically, I was early, and dressed by precisely 8 o'clock. Not early enough, apparently.

My habit of leaning into the tape caught the eye of a few of the veterans. One morning I arrived with a smile and some hellos, three minutes to spare, happy to start the day, got to my locker, and kicked off my flip-flops. No uniform. A lot of hangers but no uniform. I looked around and caught the eye of a clubbie, who shrugged. The rest of the guys were turning their chairs to the middle of the room for the start of the meeting, noticeably ignoring my little issue. Coaches filed in with clipboards and coffee cups in their hands, ready to run through the day. Everybody was in uniform, but not me.

I shot another glance at the clubbie, who shook his head and then, in an act of uncommon sympathy, glanced briefly upward. I followed his eyes and found my uniform. The jersey and pants hung from the ceiling, ten feet above my locker, like they'd been retired. That is why, in the first handful of mornings I was a Cardinal, during a team meeting, you could have found me in the equipment shed, then noisily unfolding a ladder in the clubhouse, then climbing that ladder to retrieve the clothes I had to wear that day, to the spray of helpful chatter—"All right there, Ankiel?" "You gettin' all this, Ankiel?" "Change some lightbulbs while you're up there, Ankiel?"

It didn't stop there. So I laughed plenty.

Like after early running, when we had a couple minutes to change out of our sneakers and into our cleats and trot to the next drill, only to discover the laces in my cleats had been infinitely knotted.

"You in this, Ankiel?" while I feverishly picked and pawed at my laces.

Like when the day was done and we returned to the clubhouse to clean up, only to find my shower shoes nailed to the floor.

I wore it all because I was happy to be there and it didn't feel mean, except for maybe the shower shoes.

Instructional League passed quickly. I decided I liked the Cardinals. I liked the red. I began to understand who was in all those black-and-white photos, and some of the names even matched those on the backs of jerseys that walked past. The organization's history seemed deep and fresh at the same time. The coaches didn't seem too interested in making drastic changes to my delivery, so I dug in and threw hard and spun my curveball.

In the first game, it may have been against the Cincinnati Reds, I struck out eight of nine batters. In the second, seven of nine.

I thought, and did not say out loud, *All right, this is easy.*

A few months later, at nineteen years old, I was in spring training with the major leaguers and also a handful of guys like me who tried not to get in the way. The winter in Fort Pierce had been awkward. My father had a girlfriend my mother didn't know about but Phil and I knew too much about, and in our efforts to stay neutral—or out of it completely—Mom discovered not only the girlfriend but our knowledge of her as well.

So, as usual, it was good to get out of town, leave the drama behind, and go live the game.

There was nothing about it I didn't love, even the preparation for it. Big-league camp isn't always a welcoming place for teenagers. There would be a lot of guys who'd worked long and hard for a locker in that clubhouse and maybe didn't look too kindly on those of us who'd yet to throw a professional pitch. These were grown men with wives and children and mortgages, many with long careers, some trying to squeeze another few hundred grand out of bodies that weren't so sure. I would do nothing to help the 1998 Cardinals, and yet I'd have a hook in a locker where my uniform would hang, and I'd have a place beside them at the lunch table, and a turn on the bullpen mound, and repetitions in the drills.

To fend off unnecessary judgments, I'd logged five miles almost every day in the weeks leading to the opening of camp. I was not going to be the kid who got $2.5 million the summer before and then threw up breakfast at the end of the first sprints. I arrived fit and eager and utterly awestruck that there, on the other side of the room, over lockers no bigger than mine, were placards that read "McGwire" (Mark) and "McGee" (Willie) and a dozen others I recognized.

Though I'd worn a facsimile of the uniform briefly the fall before, the first day in a real clubhouse—a spring training clubhouse, but still, surrounded by real major leaguers—buttoning that bright jersey and curling the brim of that new cap felt meaningful. This was who I'd be now. It wasn't quite my time yet, but my time was coming, and I welcomed the organization's expectations for me and my left arm. I'd keep my mouth shut. I'd throw when told to. I'd adhere to the caste system of the clubhouse. And when they said run, I'd run and then run some more.

On the first morning, the pitchers—and there were dozens of us—lined up for the first of those runs. A veteran nearby said to no one in particular, but made sure the young fellas heard, "Keep it easy. Don't be the first ones out there," meaning "No one's making the team today. There are no heroes in February." And so in the first hour of big-league camp, we ran ten five-yard sprints.

Five yards. And then rest. Then another five yards. The challenge was trying to lag behind over the course of five entire yards. But I tried.

My father called that afternoon.

"How was it?" he asked.

"Good," I said. "We did ten five-yard sprints."

"What?"

"Yep."

"Five yards?"

"Five. I'm in the best shape of my life, and we ran a total of fifty yards. In sections."

A journey of a thousand miles had begun with two steps. Slow ones. So as not to show up the veterans.

At the end of spring training, during which I'd been shipped off to minor-league camp, the Cardinals sent me to Peoria, Illinois, for A ball in the Midwest League. I was eighteen, youngest on the team by a couple years. The bus rides could be long, but I didn't mind. The towns were small, and I liked them. The ballparks were sometimes a little ratty, but mostly charming, and I was happy to be there.

I made seven starts for the Chiefs, thirty-five innings worth, and moved on, leaving behind a record for consecutive hitless innings previously held by Doc Gooden, a hero of mine as a child. The rest of my first summer was in Woodbridge, Virginia, high-A ball for the Prince William Cannons, where the fishing was decent and the baseball was the same. In 21 starts and 126 innings I struck out 181 hitters and walked 38. My fastball and curveball were playing, and my confidence was growing, and nobody was messing with my shoelaces.

Beyond that, the life fit me. For a kid whose daily existence around the baseball had been choppy for too long, the rhythms of pro ball—and nothing but pro ball—were soothing. I made my start, prepared for four days for the next one, made that start, prepared again, threw another six innings, and kept at it, and threw strikes and won ball games and made friends. If I were curious about what it would be like to stand on a field with grown men and play the game that was supposed to be my career—and I was, a little—the answer came every fifth day. Nobody pushed me off my game: I hit twelve batters and felt bad for almost none of them. My mechanics, far from classic, held up without too much maintenance.

As the Cannons rolled through Virginia, Maryland, Delaware, and North Carolina, I began to suspect I could be good at this, that my stay in the minor leagues wouldn't have to be long. It wasn't because the baseball was easy but because everything about this baseball felt right. I could commit to this. I could love it enough to be great at it, a notion I hadn't quite understood until the trees were passing on a bus bound for who knows where, with no sound but those big tires pulling us toward more baseball.

There'd been a lot of talk about the hardships of the minor leagues, where the life would thread out the weak before the baseball did. No money, except I had money. Long bus trips, except where else was I going to be? Homesickness, except I was free. Bad food, except I liked the food. Failure, except I kept striking out hitters.

Instead, I kept thinking about getting better. Getting stronger. Finding the mitt with the fastball. Getting more precise with the curveball. Washing it all down with a cold beer and moving on to the next town, see what was going on there, see if anybody was going to hit me there.

Mostly they didn't.

The drive home in September, Virginia to southern Florida, was thirteen hours. The route passed not far from a few of the ballparks I'd pitched in all summer, past "Home of the . . . " signs touting the local Class A team. I recognized some stretches I'd seen before from the other side of a bus window, eyes half open, hoping to nod off for an hour or two and instead counting backyard swing sets. It all seemed very normal from my seat, and I was happy to be out amid the normal.

I turned nineteen in the middle of that season. By the time it was over, I'd racked up 161 innings, 222 strikeouts, a 2.63 ERA, and one long drive home. If I could've stopped in Jupiter, Florida, and started the next spring training right then and there, I probably would've asked for a couple weeks but not complained much more than that. I was tired, but that good tired where you've asked something of yourself and then overdelivered.

As it was, I returned to the house I'd rented on the golf course, picked up a fishing pole, and waited to report to what would be a familiar clubhouse, if not yet mine. I'd return a minor leaguer, yes. I'd return as the kid who'd drifted through the clubhouse a year before, cast off with the early cuts while the grown men went out to do the real work. Mark McGwire hit seventy home runs that summer. Sammy Sosa hit sixty-six. They were out there saving baseball, I kept reading, and nobody was really accusing anybody of anything yet. The Yankees were becoming the best team anyone had ever seen, in spite of their second baseman, who'd contracted a mysterious ailment they called "the yips." He couldn't throw straight. No matter what he tried—arm angles, footwork, drills, eyes open, eyes closed, talking about it, not talking about it—he still had the yips. It was weird. I'd watch the highlights on television, watch his arm contort in some new way every throw, and think, *What the hell's wrong with Chuck Knoblauch? He's a good player. Just throw the ball. How's that ever happen?* Then I'd go back to breakfast and not give it another thought.

I was gaining on my own time too. I knew I was. I hoped they saw it. I'd done what I could in A ball. I'd won. I'd played hard. I'd not gotten into any trouble. I'd done as I was told.

Five months is a long time. I threw some. I ran some. Maybe not as much as I had the winter before. I figured I had those five-yarders covered. And by the time I got to Jupiter for more baseball, Baseball America had me as the game's number-two prospect. Number one would be a few lockers over: J. D. Drew. A few more people seemed to know my name. A few of the coaches would hold their gaze—and their conversations—longer. I still had a big number on my back. I still wasn't on the big-league depth chart. I was still somewhere out there, something for another day, still nineteen and learning the game. So I'd wait.

I was assigned to Double A, in Little Rock, Arkansas, where once again I'd be the only teenager in the room. But at least the bus would depart from a different parking lot and end up in different places, so I settled in for a summer of the Texas League, from Tulsa to Shreveport to San Antonio and a lot of places in between. That was good by me. Chris Maloney managed those Arkansas Travelers, and he was a good man, and there certainly would be plenty of travelin', and in that case, the more good men the better.

After eight starts in Arkansas, 49 1/3 innings' worth, I hadn't lost, my ERA was under 1, and in about six weeks I'd pitched my way out of there and into the rotation for the Triple-A Memphis Redbirds.

As the highways go, that's only about seventy miles closer to St. Louis. The way I saw it, I was a million miles closer. Just about everybody in that clubhouse had been to the big leagues or was on his way. I swear, from the top of the mound at Tim McCarver Stadium, I could almost see the lights of Busch Stadium. The Cardinals weren't very good in 1999, but it didn't yet matter to me. McGwire was still hitting about every fastball five hundred feet in St. Louis, and Drew was the regular center fielder, and a guy who'd won a World Series with a game seven walk-off hit just a couple years before—Édgar Rentería— was the shortstop, and they were in St. Louis too, where I wanted to be.

It seemed I'd spent my whole life dreaming of playing in the major leagues and working for something impossibly far away, always moving closer but never quite getting there. And then, one night, a manager named Gaylen Pitts handed me a baseball. And then I was pitching to make it to the major leagues, to take somebody's big-league job.

That baseball in my hand was as close as I'd ever been, at nineteen years old, two years from the hallways of Port St. Lucie High School, a year out of Peoria, Illinois, and I was going to throw the hell out of it.

"Just keep doin' what you've been doin'," they said, and I'd stand on those Pacific Coast League mounds and for the next three months do something like that, not a thing in my head but covering those last three hundred miles to St. Louis.

CHAPTER
TEN

On a Monday night at Olympic Stadium in Montreal, a month after my twentieth birthday, after fifty-two minor-league starts over parts of a couple summers, I made my major-league debut. The date was August 23, 1999. I'd flown to New York and been picked up at JFK Airport by a couple clubbies—Kurt Schlogl from the Cardinals and a guy they called "Icky," but whose birth certificate read Kevin Mercorella, from the Mets. Kurt was at the baggage claim, and Icky manned the car at the curb. When Kurt and I reached the passenger-side doors, the car was running, the doors were locked, and Icky—amid the commotion of cops and whistles and taxis and horns and everything else at JFK—was sound asleep. Kurt thumped the window.

"Icky!" he shouted. "Sleep when you die!"

"Nah," Icky said in an accent thick with New York. "Just resting my eyes."

So he turned to me and said, "Rick, you ever seen an asshole wrapped in plastic?"

"An asshole wrapped in plastic," I said. "Uh, no, I haven't."

Icky was laughing so hard he barely got to the punch line.

"Take a look at your driver's license."

Thanks, Icky. And welcome to the big leagues.

The Cardinals split a doubleheader at Shea Stadium— they lost on a late hit by forty-year-old Rickey Henderson in the opener and beat forty-year-old Orel Hershiser in the second game—and I tagged along to Canada.

The path, going back a bunch of years, was indirect. The baseball had been pretty good, pretty true. The world around the baseball had been a test. My mother and father sat in the dark stadium in Montreal that night, along with about thirteen thousand other folks who'd bothered to come see two teams that were about out of season.

My parents seemed proud and happy. They were, for the moment, it would appear, together, or together enough. I really tried not to ask. Some time had passed since I had pitched and they had sat together in the stands, but not so much that it felt unusual. The greatest difference, perhaps, was that I wouldn't be able to hear my father. And I would not under any circumstances be throwing a knuckleball.

The game was unremarkable for its outcome. Wearing number 66, I pitched five capable innings, and the Expos beat the Cardinals, 11–7. The remainder of the 1999 season—I'd make four more starts and three other appearances—was remarkable only for how familiar it felt. This game, one played by grown men in massive stadiums, was still played in that little rectangle they called a strike zone. The better guy won. The smarter guy lived to see another pitch. The tougher guy was standing at the end.

Six days later, I matched up against the first-place Braves, the team of my youth, and John Smoltz, whom I'd grown up wanting to be. He pitched eight innings, I pitched six, and the Braves won in twelve innings. More than forty-five thousand people were at Busch Stadium that night, which was when I began to fall in love with the city and the fans in their red caps and red shirts and red fingernails and red everything. I lived that month in a hotel room downtown and walked back from the ballpark to strangers calling my name and offering from crowded bars to buy me a beer. That I wasn't old enough to get past the bouncer occurred to none of them, which was just as well, so I waved and thought, *When's next season start?*

My fastball was hard—in the upper 90s—and reliable. My curveball earned its own nickname—"the Snapdragon," Mark McGwire called it. I was learning to pitch, a game at a time, getting it, understanding it, feeling good about where the game was taking me, even as my father was again being hauled to jail. The old-timers held me up against legends. A little wild, like a young Koufax, they said. A little mean, like Gibson at any age. The Cardinals, an organization with a proud history of legendary pitchers, seemed satisfied with the first Ankiel, maybe the next in line. I played along with the comparisons without giving them much mind, knowing the game had a way of separating the past greats from anyone who happened along with a fastball and a curveball, and maybe, just maybe, a future. It was enough to be there, to have a chance at whatever was out there every fifth night.

It was those nights when I saw only the catcher's mitt. When I heard nothing. When I was thinking, but not really thinking, *I'm going to put the ball right there*. When it was right, I was in touch with everything.

Then I'd throw the pitch. Often enough, it was right, or right enough that it'd be better the next time. The catcher—that September, Alberto Castillo or Marcus Jensen—would decide the pitch and where he wanted it and pretty soon the mounds at Busch Stadium or Wrigley Field or Turner Field began to feel like the one at Port St. Lucie High School, like they were home, and I belonged on them. That summer, in the months before I was summoned to the big leagues, I'd become consistently accurate with the fastball away from right-handed hitters, so that it could be a strike or it could tease them a few inches out of the zone or I could sink it and miss their bats entirely. That became the difference between simply overpowering minor-league hitters and competing against big-league hitters. I liked the inside fastball. In fact, I preferred the inside fastball. But it was comforting to know the outside corner was there when I needed it.

I guess I was learning how to pitch then, and learning what good hitters did to mediocre pitches and sometimes did to good pitches. And none of it felt like it was too much. I didn't feel too young or too raw. I certainly wasn't nervous. Not ever. I was not afraid, and nothing that happened over those thirty-three September innings when I was twenty nudged me from the certainty that I would show up in spring training the next year and be one of the Cardinals' five best starters, and that I would start thirty-some games, and that I'd be great at it.

Spring training is routine. Wake up at the same time every morning. Back out of the driveway at the same time. Stroll into the clubhouse at the same time. Button the top button of the jersey at the same time. Clatter across the concrete path to the field at the same time.

Players, coaches, trainers, clubbies, even the writers abided by the routine, honored the routine, built walls around the routine to ensure its purity. If the routine can be trusted today, then it can be trusted tomorrow, and one of those tomorrows would include a chartered flight out of the routine, the start of a new season, and a whole new routine. It sounds boring and tedious. It is, in fact, the only way to start in February and end in October, the only way any of that comes with success or sanity. The way to nine months of every single day was an hour at a time, a minute at a time even. Try not to look back. Definitely do not look forward, because the destination is tiny in the distance, and to chase that would be a reasonable path to exhaustion. No, just hit the next mark in the routine. Do that, and when that is done the next mark will appear. Hit them all, and at the end of the day you're fed and rested and healthy and strong and clear-headed and confident. Miss one, then another, and that day gets wobbly, and the next is too full trying to cover for the previous one, and the next is messier, and this is how sore elbows and bad Aprils and doubt and stomachaches are born.

I gazed at my father's back in that spring of 2000, and what was going through my mind was not that he'd hoisted himself from his chair in a courthouse in Fort Pierce to stand before the judge who would sentence him for his crimes but what was happening to my daily routine. What tomorrow would be as a result. What I'd do, whom I'd have to talk to, where I'd go, all to catch up, all to get back on schedule.

I was sure I would make the Cardinals' rotation out of spring training. I'd pitched well enough the previous September to know whatever talent I had would play in the big leagues and that whatever I needed to learn could happen there, around big-league players, and not in Memphis. In order to do that, however, I'd have to be there and around big-league players, not taking a day off to sit next to my mother on a wooden bench just to show a judge that one Richard Ankiel had loving family and people who believed in his rehabilitative potential, none of which the judge probably believed anyway.

I gazed at my father's back. He was going to jail for a long time, and everyone would know that when I'd told them he was a drywaller that was only part of it, and I'd be the guy in jail's kid, and I thought, *Hell, there's worse things.* No more crazy phone calls from the old man, I wrongly thought. No more worrying about Mom. Wrong again. No more burying the truth. I didn't wish prison on him, but the benefits of it weren't lost on me either. Life was about to get really shitty for him. There was part of me that felt bad about that, even if by any measure he'd had it coming. And life was about to get a little softer, a little calmer, for the rest of us. For months my father had been edgy even by his standards, convinced he'd be offed by the Bahamians he'd screwed over or by friends of the handful of others he'd screwed over, so we added paranoia to his list of personality traits. Then there'd been this federal agent, a woman, who'd guided him through the process of rolling over on his former partners—these were the people he believed would surely cut his car's brake lines now—and he became convinced that she had fallen for him. Like, romantically. And I—a kid who had not the vaguest idea of how any of this worked but had watched enough TV to know when a scammer was getting scammed, by a cop no less—turned away so as not to laugh directly in his face.

My father was going to jail for five years or thirty or something in between. My half-brother, Phil, was already in the system, in a cell somewhere because, basically, he'd drifted into Dad's line of work. So I sat beside my mother, who wasn't any happier to be there than I was, and we waited for the inevitable, and while we did I had the thought that having a father who smuggled drugs and waved guns around like a redneck Scarface might actually work for me. I wasn't just some twenty-year-old rookie with a fastball and a tough-guy act. The shit I'd seen, that I'd put up with, that I'd lived alongside and defended my-self against—that was real. That left scars. Think some baseball game at Shea Stadium is scary? Try staying one room ahead of a lousy-drunk father pissed because you swung at ball four in an American Legion game. Try getting caught and made to run laps for it. Try being the one telling your mom it's fine, it's OK, because if she stepped in I'd be picking her up off the floor too. Try finding bags of pot where the toilet paper should be or dustings of coke on the kitchen counter and then being told *you're* the good-for-nothing idiot.

In the game you make your reputation a pitch at a time. Keep showing up, keep doing your job, keep making the right decisions, keep getting outs, keep standing out there without fear or hesitation. That's a gamer. But, hey, if some hitter wants to hold in his head somewhere that I'm a little tougher than he is, that I'll fight if I have to, that I've had a life that didn't look anything like his, then maybe that buys me an inch or two on the inside corner. Maybe that gets him rocking back off the plate, and maybe he doesn't even know it. Just his instinct telling him it'd be best to give this one a little extra room.

It was a dumb notion, probably. But I'd believe it for a while. If my father was going to distract me from being the ballplayer and the man I wanted to be because of his presence, then I figured he could at least be useful in his absence. The details of his crimes and then his punishment would be in the newspapers, and the Cardinals would ask why I hadn't told them and I would answer that I didn't think it was important. Reporters would slip in questions about my father, somewhere between how my arm felt and if that changeup was coming around, and I'd let my face get serious and tell them, "People make mistakes. He made a mistake." I wasn't sorry people knew. I didn't care. He wasn't me. He hadn't been for a very long time. He wouldn't ever be me again.

I gazed at my father's back and thanked him for making me a harder person and a meaner pitcher. I thanked him for the reputation I probably didn't deserve.

He stood behind the table next to his lawyer and the judge looked down at him, then at some notes, then back at him.

Dad got six years.

I stood up, walked out of the courtroom, gave my mother a hug, and drove back to Jupiter so I could be a big-league pitcher, rep or not.

That spring, after enough of Scott Boras's urging and my conclusion that it would be the only way for him to stop harping on it, I agreed to meet Harvey Dorfman, a man with a rep of his own. He was a sports psychologist. I'd heard of those guys. Not by name or anything, but the fact that they were around, that one of them had even worn a Florida Marlins uniform and sat on their bench while they were winning the World Series. Turned out, that was Harvey. Some of the older players, I'd learned, were big on the mental side of the game, which was fine, but I figured I was set there. I'd spent my whole life, such as it was, exploring new ways to shut people out.

"Just talk to him," Scott said. "He's a good guy. You'll like him."

"I'm good," I said. "Nah."

But Scott would not let it go, and one afternoon I had an hour free, and Harvey was in Jupiter, and if an hour with Harvey meant even one fewer conversation with

Scott about how good a guy Harvey was, it would be worth it. So I knocked on a hotel-room door and a sixty-five-year-old balding man with dark circles under his eyes opened it. OK, this was gonna be awkward.

"I'm Rick," I said.

"Harvey," he said.

I walked into the room, looked around, and said, "All right, so do I lay down on the fucking couch or something or what?"

He laughed like he'd heard it before and gestured toward a chair.

I'd been lied to my whole life. I trusted no one except me. Give me the ball, make me no promises, stay out of the way. That's the lens through which I eyed Harvey, and answered his easy questions, and wondered when I could leave.

It was fine. He seemed a decent guy. He was warm and smart. He was curious without pushing too hard. On my way out, in spite of my reservations, I asked if he played golf. It was supposed to sound like an invitation, a way to continue the relationship without really committing to it, in case he didn't want to. Maybe out of duty to Scott. Maybe because I liked the man, if I had no use for his skills. Maybe he knew that.

"A little," he said.

I nodded. We both knew we probably wouldn't be playing any golf.

As I walked down the hallway, I considered the previous hour. I was the toughest guy I knew. I was twenty years old, and life, finally, was great. I'd worked for that.

Where had somebody like this been eight years ago, when I was picking my mom off the floor? Seven years ago, when I was saying good-bye to Dennis? I could've used some answers then. But now? What did I need with a head doctor? I'd fixed that.

Yeah, good guy, this Harvey Dorfman. And I'd probably never see him again.

The Cardinals of seventy-five wins and a fourth-place National League Central finish in 1999 would become the Cardinals of ninety-five wins and a first-place National League Central finish in 2000. In the off-season, they'd traded for Darryl Kile. Freed from the thin air of Denver and Coors Field, he won twenty games and was an All Star. Mark McGwire played half the season and hit thirty-two home runs. Jim Edmonds played the whole season, hit forty-two home runs, and was an All Star. Fernando Viña hit .300. Mike Matheny, the veteran catcher with a reputation for intelligence and professionalism, signed as a free agent and was better than his reputation. Eric Davis, at thirty-eight, hit .303, and J. D. Drew, at twenty-four, hit .295. Will Clark, at thirty-six, hit .345 in a third of a season. The starting rotation was veterans—Kile, Garrett Stephenson, Pat Hentgen, Andy Benes—and me.

Kile, who'd made his major-league debut as a twenty-two-year-old a decade before, was especially kind. By then, he'd won a lot and lost plenty too, so he had a way of seeing the game and then imparting insight that was authentic and encouraging. I was raw in spots and a little wild at times—ten strikeouts over six innings in my first start became five walks in five innings in my second and another seven walks in five innings of my third—but that didn't bother Darryl.

"You're right there, Ank," he'd say. "An inch here or there."

Dave Duncan, the pitching coach, didn't say much and Mike Matheny had a dozen other pitchers to tend to. So I'd sit and listen to Darryl, and he'd ask questions about this pitch or that one, and I began to understand that there needed to be a good reason to throw that pitch in that situation to that hitter to that spot, and Mike wasn't going to be there to call every pitch for the rest of my life.

That season—every at bat against every hitter in every city, the wins and the losses, the dumb mistakes and the flashes of clarity—was to prepare me for twenty years of this. Darryl reminded me every day, in his words and just by being there and caring.

"What'd you learn today?" he'd ask.

"A high fastball sure does carry," I'd say.

He'd laugh, and we'd move on to the next scouting report, a list of guys I'd heard of but not pitched against, and then a couple days later I'd go throw a hundred pitches and see how that went.

Darryl was smart, and he saw things in a baseball game hardly anyone else saw. He worked so hard he made an entire pitching staff stronger and more prepared, because no one wished to be viewed as a slacker in comparison, though some days it was difficult not to be. He possessed a natural curiosity for what worked on a pitcher's mound and what didn't, and when he decided he wanted a new pitch to go along with his fastball and curveball, by the next spring he had a forkball that was among the best in the game. Darryl took the ball and made his starts and pitched his innings, because that's what a pitcher was supposed to do, and he did not gripe about the heat or his shoulder being sore or the offense not getting him enough runs. He was the guy you wanted to sit next to on the bench for three hours during a game, then sit next to at a bar for an hour afterward, so he could tell you what you'd just seen for three hours.

Darryl and his wife, Flynn, had two young children—a boy and girl, they were twins—and he talked about them often. He was eleven years older than I was, and while he had a family he adored and a job that took up most of his time, he found time for me and my career, and in many ways I wanted to grow up to be just like Darryl Kile. I wanted to be a good man. He wasn't the next Sandy Koufax, but I'd have taken the life he had if I could.

Nearing the end of August, Darryl and I were pitching one day apart from each other. First him, then me. I watched him pitch toward twenty wins at the end of a long season. They're all long. He seemed to get stronger, and he found ways out of difficult spots, and in his final seven starts Darryl was 6–0 with a 2.72 ERA. I'd come in behind him on the next night, and in those seven starts I was 4–0 with a 1.97 ERA. On September 20 I beat the Houston Astros and the Cardinals clinched the division, and a week later I won my eleventh game. I'd finish 11–7 with a 3.50 ERA, my first season behind me, the playoffs six days ahead. That I'd ended so well, that the trials of the season had made me better, that the coaching staff's confidence in me seemed to match the confidence I had in myself, I thought, meant the best was coming. First the Braves in the division series and then whoever came after them, and then the better part of a lifetime after that. I was ready.

Scott Boras told me I'd start game one of the playoffs against the Braves. He was guessing, but his logic seemed sound. Because there would be an off day between the first and second games, the pitcher who started game one could pitch game four on regular rest, that being four days. The gap between games two and five was three days. I'd not started on three days' rest as a professional. Darryl had, plenty. I was twenty-one years old, and even before the notions of hard innings and pitch limits had taken hold in the league, people were smart enough to have figured out the longer the rest, the safer (and stronger) the arm. Then, the Braves had been tough on Darryl in two starts. They'd not seen me since the September before, thirteen months before, and in the meantime I'd put nearly two hundred big-league innings on my arm and into my head and introduced a sinker that darted away from righthanders. No one was more sure of himself than I was.

The counterargument to me in game one? Because Darryl Kile, that's why. He was the ace, undisputedly. He was a grown-up with playoff experience. A month before, he'd allowed two runs in a complete-game win against the Braves in Atlanta. Andy Benes had something wrong with his hand, Garrett Stephenson's elbow was sore, and Pat Hentgen seemed worn out. That left Darryl and me.

Tony La Russa and Dave Duncan had penciled out a rotation that had me starting game one. They slept on it for a night. Then two. Tony wondered about putting so much on a twenty-one-year-old, a rookie. He believed there was a risk of too much too soon and whatever might come of that. I didn't believe it, though. I wanted the ball. And by Monday morning—the day after our final regular-season game and the day before we'd open the division series against the Braves—the lure of having Darryl and me cover four of those games was too much to pass up. If the series went five games, I would pitch games one and four. Darryl would pitch games two and, on three days' rest, five. With everybody else a little banged up or gassed, that would leave only game three to be covered, and that went to Garrett.

Still, Tony remained bothered. He would, by this plan, get the most from his two healthiest arms. But, he asked himself, what of the larger burden on me, the rookie? So, on Monday, he announced that Darryl Kile would start game one, and Darryl answered the media's questions that afternoon about facing the Braves knowing he would not be the starter the next afternoon, that I would. This was Tony's plan to relieve some of the pressure. That night he called Atlanta's manager, Bobby Cox, and told him they'd made a switch, that Ankiel—not Kile—would start Tuesday.

"Rick's got enough on him," he told Bobby, and Bobby thanked him for the call.

The Cardinals later sent out a release to reporters, notifying them of the change—which wasn't a change but part of the plan all along.

That's what I walked into Tuesday morning, October 3, 2000. Not that I cared. Tony and Dave knew what they were doing. If Darryl was disappointed, he didn't say so. And the Braves were not at a disadvantage. The media believed they had been duped, and the fans who had gone to bed thinking they'd see Darryl the next afternoon were confused. None of it registered with me. I knew I'd miss Mike Matheny, my regular catcher, but I'd pitch on five days' rest, one more than usual, I'd pitch at home, and I was pitching better than I ever had. Give me the ball and get out of the way.

I had an apartment in Clayton, a suburb west of St. Louis, on the other side of a large green park that had museums and a zoo I never went to. My mom was in town for the first two games of the series. She stayed with me. We drove to the ballpark hours before first pitch. I left her to fill that time on her own and made my way to the clubhouse, little in my head but what a great day this would be, feeling young and invincible. I also was wondering how many hits I might get off Greg Maddux. At my locker I drew out a bat and felt it in my hands, waggled it, took some easy swings. A voice behind me laughed and said, "You're always worried about hitting." Not worried, though. Excited. I enjoyed pitching. I was good at it. I loved to hit.

I'd batted .250 that season, which I thought was pretty decent for a guy who hardly ever hit anymore. I homered twice in the same week in April so pretty much tried to jack everything after that. We won both of those games and I didn't give up a run in either, so I figured it was good luck for my pitching if I hit a home run. I tried a lot.

I stood there half dressed and half listening to the chatter of a clubhouse coming alive, a black Rawlings bat cocked behind my left ear and thinking about fastballs—Maddux's, not mine. Satisfied with that, I leaned the gamer bat against the side of the locker, slid a pair of headphones over my ears, and got to thinking about being a pitcher. Or at least acting like being a pitcher. My routine started with a nap, maybe forty minutes, in the trainer's room, which never failed to amuse some of the veteran Cardinals. I trusted Dave Duncan's scouting report, and I trusted myself even if a game started to stagger away from that scouting report, and I trusted that I was a better pitcher than any of those other guys—today the Braves—were hitters. I slept well.

There's something ceremonial about sliding the game jersey from its hanger, slipping into it, and then buttoning it. And then it was time. The headphones were gone. The clubbie had gathered up the bat and run it through the tunnel to the rack in the dugout with the rest of the bats. The time had come to pitch, to check in with my body, to stretch and throw long in the outfield, to finish in the bullpen, to feel the ballpark fill up and somewhere in my peripheral vision see the stands turn red and somewhere in the distance hear my name in the mouths of those people, louder on that day because they'd expected Darryl Kile. We'd won ninety-five games. We were a good team. Eighteen years had passed since the last Cardinals' World Series championship, most of a generation had passed, and folks get impatient. The Braves had won ninety-five too. We'd have to play well, and we knew we would, starting that day, starting with that first pitch, starting with me.

In the bullpen, we'd start with fastballs on my arm side of the plate. That is, away from right-handed hitters. Then to the other side of the plate. Some curveballs. Then we'd pick a couple guys from their lineup—Chipper Jones, the switch-hitter, a righty against me, for one—and simulate an at bat. Strike one. Ball one. Foul ball. Ball two. Finish him with the curveball, always finishing with a strikeout, always with a *thwack* of the catcher's mitt and a nod and an "All right, let's go" and a lot of positive thoughts.

My game. October. Playoffs. I walked from the bullpen to the dugout, staring at the ground a few yards ahead, aware of the grass under my feet but not really seeing it, aware of a ballpark thumping with music and laughter but not really hearing it. If there's a baseball equivalent to the boxer's entrance, this was it, without the guys bouncing around in the background or the glittery shorts. I'd be so deep into my psyche, seeing but not seeing, that sometimes I'd be surprised by the top step of the dugout.

It was weird, a little, that all this would come against the Braves, my favorite team until about my third day as a Cardinal. Growing up, I could recite their lineup and do a reasonable batting impression of most of them. In game one, their leadoff hitter was Rafael Furcal, who in a few weeks would win the National League Rookie of the Year award. I'd be second. Behind him in the order was Andruw Jones, who four years before had hit two home runs in the first game of the World Series against the Yankees, making me about the happiest kid in Fort Pierce. Then Chipper Jones, Andrés Galarraga, Brian Jordan, Reggie Sanders, Walt Weiss, Paul Bako, and Greg Maddux. I knew of them all. Some were Braves heroes, so formerly my heroes, and for this afternoon the men who would learn my name.

My command wasn't great, not like it had been in recent weeks, but my fastball was hard and curveball biting. In the first inning, Furcal singled. I struck out Andruw Jones. While I was in the process of walking Chipper Jones on five pitches, Furcal was thrown out trying to steal second. With Jones on first, I walked Galarraga. Jordan popped out to first baseman Will Clark in foul territory. No damage, but twenty-three pitches, which were too many. I could feel my adrenaline running hot, and I sat on the bench telling myself to settle down, that it was just another ball game.

As I held this conversation with myself, we scored six runs off Maddux. I even got my at bat in the first inning, thinking home run, of course, and popped to shortstop. Six runs against Maddux didn't happen often, certainly not all in the same inning, certainly not in the first inning, but the boys were fired up and attacking Maddux early in the count, hunting get-ahead fastballs, and there we were—there I was—ahead 6–0 before the turnstiles at the stadium had stopped spinning.

Encouraged by that, I bounced off the bench for the second inning, put another zero on the scoreboard with only eleven pitches, and returned to the dugout, thinking, *Two down. Seven more to go. Keep 'er goin'.*

We put two more runners on base against Maddux in the bottom of the second inning. Neither scored. Along came the third inning.

I swept up my glove and headed for the mound. Nothing could beat me now.

CHAPTER
ELEVEN

For something like twenty years, counting every ball I picked up and heaved as a two-year-old, every down-and-out I ran in the street in front of my house, every basketball I tossed toward a playground rim, sports were size, speed, muscle, skill, and, if they had to be, practice. Sports were being a little meaner. Maybe a little taller. Sports were throwing harder, and making contact, and making a play, bleeding a little and hanging tough anyway. Sports were loud and in your face and . . . out there, where everybody could see.

Sports were played over huge open spaces—fields, gyms, stadiums. The games of my youth and early adulthood were decided across those spaces, with my arm and my bat, wielded by thick legs and shoulders, and because of that I was better. I could run and jump and I had arm speed and bat speed. I worked. I worked more. I ran. I grew stronger. I grew faster. And I loved it so hard, needed it so badly, that it loved me back, which inspired me to run harder and play better. Sports drew me out of my own head, from my insecurities and fears, my suspicion that I was the person my dad must think I was, because otherwise why would he say that stuff to me? Why would he be so angry?

In some ways sports raised me, and their advice along the way leaned to the cutthroat. *Take care of you. Get away from all that noise.* They asked me if I were tough enough. They asked me if I were man enough. *Here's a glove and here's a ball. Now what kind of a person are you? What is your worth? In all this space, who are you? What are you?*

There would be talk of "game faces." Of "focus." Of "the zone." But, really, in those days when I was clear of mind and ferocious of heart, the entire ballpark would narrow to the width of a baseball. OK, so who's going to win those final few inches? Who really wants to win? Which one of you loses and trudges back to Fort Pierce, a failure, and into that house where the memories would come back to life, where the nightmares live?

Those games were won by the hiss of a fastball, the *foomp* of a catcher's mitt, the bellow of an umpire. That was what fair-and-square sounded like. I stand here. You stand there. Play ball. That was sports.

Clinically, I believe, what happened is this: I dunno. And neither does anyone else. They can tell you they do. They don't. They can guess. Doesn't mean it's true.

One moment, I was a pitcher. The next, I was a patient. A project. A cautionary tale. A lab rat. A fairly mis-
erable human being. I was, quite suddenly, my father's
son. A casualty of the game, of a broken family, of a heart-
less world, of all the stuff that may or may not have been
swirling around in my head.

I drew back my arm, and it was the last time I wouldn't
think about that.

With a single throw I'd joined the List.

Steve Blass.

Chuck Knoblauch.

Mark Wohlers.

Steve Sax.

Mackey Sasser.

On and on.

. . . Rick Ankiel.

Ready?

It's an anxiety disorder. No, it's "misplaced focus." Unless it's plain old "performance anxiety," which, I suppose,
is something very close to "choking," except nobody likes
that word.

Your brain quit on you. Unless, and this was something to think about, your brain knew best, and it really
was *protecting* you. You don't want to throw this pitch, it's
not going to end well, so I won't *let* you throw it.

It's a neurological disorder. Narrower? How about
"focal dystonia," in which one's muscles contract invol-
untarily? Broader? The old-time golfers called it "the
yips." Older-time than that? "Whiskey fingers." Yes, it is

neurological. Unless it is psychological. Or physical. Or all of it, all balled up into one large sob.

Damn, man, just pick up the ball and throw it.

Johnny Miller, the golfer, once told *Golf Digest* in a moment of vulnerability, "I have a wire corroded in my head."

It's an organic disease of the brain, except it's never shown up in an autopsy. It's learned, unlearned, and learned again. It's visible in life, invisible in death, and I don't know after that.

It's ballplayers, archers, piano players, darts players, free-throw shooters, cricket bowlers, putters, quarterbacks, even writers.

It's not physical, it's mental. It's a small seizure. It's a medium seizure. That sounds physical. It's not a seizure at all. It's a spark of fear, of humiliation, of regret before the fact. That sounds mental.

It's genetic. They think it could be genetic! You know what it's not? Genetic, I'm guessing.

The science is somewhat split on the cause of the yips, which is why everyone calls it "the Thing," which is what it'll be called even if someone does come up with a sturdy, accurate, and learned description of the condition that turns ballplayers into plumbers. Besides, "whiskey fingers" is taken.

It's the Thing because it is both there and not, real and mystical, and because it sounds like it could've dragged itself out of the ooze (in this case, of one's head) and gotten to feeding on the children of the townsfolk.

There are victims. Hypotheses have been formed, studies have been undertaken, and conclusions have been drawn.

There is, however, little agreement. There is only slight overlap between different ideas.

It began the moment I let go of the last pitch I ever truly trusted, the one that went to the backstop and changed my life, and in the few seconds that followed. What happened to me? What snagged in my brain? Was it an emotional response? A physical one? A chemical one? An electrical one? Was it born of a father-son relationship that spoiled, then curled up in my head waiting for the least opportune (for me) moment to present itself?

Was I vulnerable? Weren't we all?

Four decades ago, Steve Blass told Roger Angell in the *New Yorker* of the moment he let go of the last pitch he ever believed in: "It was just one of the awfulest games and awfulest nights I've ever had in my life. . . . I knew there was something tragically, tragically wrong here. And I am lost here, and I do not have a clue what I'm doing. I wind up, and there's kind of this freeze, and there's no flow and no rhythm. I knew I shouldn't be out there, but I didn't want to quit. I wanted to keep going to be totally convinced that it wasn't there."

That was me too. And that was it—the fight against the invisible, the shapeless. The fight had turned inward, against myself.

Forty years after Steve Blass's awfulest night, the Thing is just as mysterious. Maybe more. We've had forty years to find its soft spot. Instead, it grows harder. Meaner. It doesn't just beat ballplayers and pianists and free-throw shooters, it beats scientists and psychiatrists and psychologists. It beats everyone. It's damned near undefeated.

What the hell is this thing?

Dr. Mark Oakley is a clinical psychologist, a full clinical professor at University of California–Los Angeles and the founder and director of the Center for Cognitive Therapy, which has offices in Beverly Hills, California, and Diamond Bar, California. He consults with UCLA sports teams. He has a son who plays baseball.

We spoke in the summer of 2016, coming up on sixteen years after the wire in my head corroded, which is not the precise technical phraseology. I had not thrown a professional pitch in twelve years. Why not? Why had I lost the one thing that most defined me, all at once? Even in the darkest of hours, when the yips threatened to consume me, the reason for my affliction was, I believed, irrelevant. It happened. It wouldn't let go. During all those years, I knew that if I were to pitch again—not merely survive but pitch—the more critical question was not why but how. How it worked, how I could work around it, how to tame the monster. Twelve years later, when pitching was no longer an option, the question "Why?" had become, at the least, a curiosity. To my surprise, I discovered that young players in the throes of performance anxiety, some of it severe, would be prone to asking "Why?" or even "Why me?"

I answered the only way I could, the only way I knew. That was "I don't know why."

So, while driving my boys to the water park one morning, I called Dr. Oakley and asked him. Why?

Why the yips?

Why some people and not others?

Why the easy stuff? The routine throws?

Why, if it can be contracted so easily, can it not be cured as easily? Why, if it can be summoned in a single pitch, can it not be buried in two or three or a thousand?

"The yips," he said, "can be explained in both psychological and neuromuscular terms, and it's extremely complicated. It's very difficult to treat and very difficult to understand. . . . What it boils down to, a mistake is made, ultimate trust is eroded, pressure interferes with the lack of trust, and that compounds the problem. Now there's anxiety, and a vicious cycle ensues."

Along come the obsessive thoughts, Dr. Oakley said, the failure, the pursuit of perfection now fouled by anxiety and more failure and more anxiety.

"This," he added, "is a phenomenon on steroids."

I asked if a particular type of person, and the athlete within that person, were more prone to the failure-anxiety-failure merry-go-round, still thinking of "Why?"

"I wouldn't be surprised," he said. "There could be people with predispositions. That said, everybody in the right circumstances might be susceptible to it, and all the anxiety disorders"—here he mentioned obsessive-compulsive disorder—"have things in common. That is, the arousal that comes with it. That's the common denominator."

So which comes first, the mistake or the anxiety? Which causes the other?

"I would have to say it's probably an interplay between the two," he said. "The changes are physiological.

Adrenaline, heart rate, blood pressure. And then it's that classic fight-or-flight mechanism engaging. Between the two, the system starts locking up."

Ball one, ball two, ball three . . .

"I've taken a paradoxical approach," Dr. Oakley said. "First, know there is no cure. Anybody who tells you otherwise is being misleading."

The typical treatment, in my experience, was to ward off the feelings of anxiety, which, exposed and left to bubble, led to full-blown panic and embarrassing results. I practiced every day, nearly all day, to tamp the rumblings of uncertainty. I built walls against the approaching forces that surely would wreck the fastball I'd have to throw in eight hours. Those were the breathing exercises, the attempts to distract myself and drive whatever was surfacing back inside. Nearly every time, those walls would fall at the first sign of peril. What I'd think later was *Bigger walls. I need bigger walls. And a moat.*

The focus, then, was to manage what was going on. The keywords were *focus, eliminate distractions*, and, my favorite, *relax.*

Just throw the ball, Rick. . . .

"When a person's really distressed, they're overwhelmed by that," Dr. Oakley said. "Turn it on its head. Instead of curtailing that moment, bring it on. Experience that. Spend more time with it.

"Most people, of course, don't want to spend time with it. It's not a pleasant thing. So what I do, and it goes along with treating anxiety disorders, I try prolonged exposure to it. You actually need more time with it, what my friend Ken Ravizza calls 'getting comfortable with being uncomfortable.'"

A narrative is developed, Dr. Oakley explained, that re-creates for the afflicted the physical occurrence that sparked the psychological reaction. So, for example, if a pitcher began throwing baseballs to the backstop and suffered, as a result, a panic attack right there on the mound, that pitcher's psyche would be brought back to that moment—the sights, the sounds, the feel of the ball off his fingertips, and then the physical and emotional reactions to that pitch. That is, Dr. Oakley reconstructs the inaugural exposure to the yips so that the response is similar.

Maybe that requires ninety minutes or longer, and the patient spends time in that horribly uncomfortable place, over and over, living and reliving an experience he—or she—has typically attempted and failed to forget. The yips sufferer is provided a tape whereby he may summon his fears at will, and live with them again, and soak himself in the experience.

On the field, when the world went sideways and I turned to my relaxation techniques, I found that they invariably fed my already growing anxiety. By turning my attention away from the hitter, away from the strike zone, away from the game, and to myself, my own problems, I'd acknowledged there was an issue. And the issue was me.

"It's the same thing," Dr. Oakley said, "if we have someone who fears elevators. We have them spend time in elevators. If they have a fear of heights, we spend time at heights. Until they stop responding to it. A lot of prolonged and repetitious time and you basically get sick of it."

When the panic comes, and it will come, the patient already has been there, and been there a lot, and perhaps it does not seem as scary or hopeless. Maybe, even, the whole thing is a little boring.

"Does it work?" I asked.

Sometimes, he said. "I try to help," he said. "Sometimes I can't. But there are people I do help. Then, rather than demanding excellence, like it's all or nothing, they are free to pursue excellence."

There are stories of recovery. Steve Sax survived his battle with the yips. Jarrod Saltalamacchia, the big-league catcher, revealed he'd used a technique called "tapping," clearing negative emotion by touching parts of his body with his fingers, to overcome a fear of throwing to the pitcher. Mackey Sasser left the game, lived in a trailer on a beach for long enough to ease the stress, then found peace and a reliable arm stroke while coaching college players. Even Steve Blass, long after he retired, found a method to relieve his throwing anxieties, if only for a few glorious days when he was fifty-five years old. Sometimes that's enough. Sometimes it has to be.

There are ways, I suppose, to fool the brain into believing all is well, that the mystery is solved, and that the body should follow. Still, the Thing is lost in there somewhere, locked in a place that is neither fully brain nor arm, that is both.

It does not ever leave, even when rebuilt. The ashes remain.

Dr. Ken Ravizza has been a sports psychologist for four decades. Men and women, boys and girls, fathers and mothers, sons and daughters, the afflictions of doubt and fear and anxiety that come with the games touch them all, and for that Ravizza has adopted the chilling adage "You go and you stand naked before the gods."

Be they Olympic gods, golf gods, or baseball gods, or parents, coaches, or fans, be they television cameras or press-box hounds, they regard the worthy and unworthy with the same grave countenance. Play the games. Play them honestly. Do not tremble. Do not stumble. Do not fail.

Now, go have fun.

I'd go to the ballpark, throw, do what I needed to do in the weight room, and then for the next twenty-two hours I'd be in my hotel room, by myself, driving myself crazy. I was very lonely, and very scared.

—Mark Wohlers, 1998, *New York Times*

I don't need this. I'm not out here for the money. I'm out here to have fun. I don't need the money. I don't need this.

—Chuck Knoblauch, 2000

I remember walking into the clubhouse in San Diego, slamming my glove into the locker and seriously considering quitting at something for the only time in my life. I mean, it was almost like I was a prisoner to it. I'd wake up with it, go to bed with it and feel it in my stomach when I ate. Everybody made fun of me. I was the laughingstock of the league.

—Steve Sax, 1999, *Los Angeles Times*

I know my problem strikes some people as absurd. At least once a day, some friend, casual acquaintance or perhaps even a stranger who recognizes me will say, "Why is it that you can't get the ball over the plate? It seems so simple."

So simple. That noise you just heard was what's left of my hollow laugh.

—Rex Barney, 1954, *Collier's Weekly*

Who does this happen to? It's someone who cares a lot.

—Harvey Dorfman, 2001, *Houston Chronicle*

"And," Dr. Ravizza said, "you still have to go out there and perform."

Naked, before the gods.

"I have not found the cure," he said. "I think it's different for each person. It's not black or white but gray. . . . For me, I talk about it first as an arm issue. Maybe there's a tweak, keep it in that area. That at least buys a little time before we go to the dark side."

He recalled speaking with a long-forgotten baseball prospect, a catcher who hit well enough to make a career of the game and lost that career when he could not throw a ball accurately farther than his own shadow. The organization brought in a sports psychologist, who told the prospect right off, "This is a critical situation, and it's going to determine whether you get to the big leagues or not."

"Ken," he said, "whatever you do, never tell anyone that."

"I'll take that advice," he answered.

There are more of them now than ever, Dr. Ravizza said, and I believe that. In my year with the Washington Nationals, traveling the major and minor leagues, I saw them. Some were on the verge. Others were full-blown. A few would say hello, talk around the subject, and take my card. Eventually, they'd call. When the booze didn't work, when the anger wasn't enough, when the self-pity outran the resolve to "handle this," and when the nightmares came, they'd call.

"Yeah," I'd say, "I know. I know."

By then, everybody knew.

"Whoo, it's a hard one," Dr. Ravizza said. "First thing, they may get through this, they might not get through this. People do get through this. And I admire their courage. Whatever the result, it's something—this courage—they'll take with them through their lives, that's a part of their character, a part of who they are."

CHAPTER
TWELVE

On the afternoon of October 3, 2000, Steve Blass sat in his favorite chair in the living room of his house in Pittsburgh. A baseball game was on the television. He still loved baseball, stubbornly.

The game was televised from St. Louis. He'd done some pitching himself so was eager to see the great Greg Maddux, who on his best days ran a game with marionette strings. The ball behaved when Greg Maddux threw it. Against Maddux, for the Cardinals, pitched the young left-hander everyone seemed to think so much of.

Steve Blass wouldn't ever forget that game, which would make two of us.

In his chair, he winced. His heart rate quickened. He'd seen a million wild pitches. He'd seen this, what was happening on his television screen, this emotional distress, once before. That time, it was him.

"Oh, my God," he said aloud to no one. "Oh, my God, I know. This is terrible. A terrible thing."

He looked into my face, twenty-one years old. He saw calm. He knew better.

"Why at the beginning?" he said. "Why now?"

His wife, Karen, looked up. She'd lived it as well.

"I hope this isn't what I think it is," he said to her. "At least mine was at the end. Shit, if he doesn't get over this, he's not going to have those things, those wonderful things we had, remember, Karen? Playing for all those years, playing with all those guys . . . "

He knew, though. It was exactly what he thought it was.

The phone rang. It was a writer from Pittsburgh, a man he'd known for decades.

"You watching this?" the man asked.

"I'm watching. It's not any fun either."

Steve Blass won 103 games from 1964 to 1974, all for the Pittsburgh Pirates. He beat the Baltimore Orioles twice in the 1971 World Series, including in Game 7, a 2–1, complete-game masterwork that brought him icon status in Pittsburgh.

In addition to being a good pitcher—he won at least fifteen games four times and in 1972 won a career-high nineteen, finishing second to Steve Carlton in the Cy Young Award balloting—Blass loved his work. He was a cutup in the clubhouse. He was known to throw a complete game, receive the ball from his catcher, then pass the ball to a young fan on his way from the field. He even enjoyed talking to reporters, calling them over for laughs and long conversations after games. Few appreciated baseball or their place in it the way Blass did. It wasn't just a job for him, which made the end especially cruel.

I met Steve in July 2015. He was seventy-three years old. He smiled, shook my hand, and led me into a basement room across the hall from the visitors' clubhouse at PNC Park in Pittsburgh. Steve worked as a television analyst for Pirates games. The cramped, sloped-ceilinged room served as an office for the broadcast crew, but really it was a place to plug in a small refrigerator for the postgame beers.

"I've been looking forward to sitting down," he said, "because nobody knows like we do."

I nodded. I thought I was looking forward to it too. I hoped I was. It wasn't easy bringing back the worst parts of my past, willingly chasing horrible memories I'd pushed away for so long. My instinct was to let them lie in the ditch I'd left them in a decade before.

As it happened, the Cardinals were in the visitors' clubhouse across the hall. Fifteen years after he'd sliced up his hand and then watched from the dugout rail as I came undone, Mike Matheny was in the manager's office, thinking through the night's lineup. I'd gone in to say hello, brushing as I did against the familiar road grays I'd last worn six years before.

The day I met Steve in Pittsburgh, not forty feet from the door that led to the Cardinals, I was thirty-five years old, younger than some of the men in that room, still spitting distance from my prime. But I was retired, twice over. As they prepared for a baseball game in what would become a pennant race and a one-hundred-win season, I'd settle into an old office chair, seeking a clue as to why I was on the wrong side of the hallway.

Steve hadn't thrown a significant pitch in more than forty years. He was older than my father. He retired at thirty-two, barely two years after winning nineteen games and four years before I was born, because he couldn't throw strikes anymore. A quarter of a century later, I caught what had become named for him: Steve Blass Disease.

That is, the sudden inability to do what you've done for your whole life, and to have that failure play in front of the whole world . . . day after day after day. And then you go home. That's the antidote—an Adirondack chair on the back porch.

Steve had watched from a distance the day my career died. It would be an extended death, and I would fight like hell to stop it, but it was inevitable. He said he had wanted to reach out, to come closer, to tell me his story so maybe I wouldn't feel so alone. Every time, he'd stopped himself. He'd asked himself what would be the use. There'd already be enough inside my head, Steve knew. I wouldn't need him in there too. And there was no cure, none that he knew of, so what would he have said? He laughed to himself, remembering the remedies that had come by mail to Riverfront Stadium, in care of the guy who couldn't throw straight. Four-leaf clovers, they'd said. Crosses, of course. Looser underwear, they'd recommended. He'd tried that last one.

Blass was not the first to contract the Thing, only the one they named it after, and so I went to Pittsburgh looking for answers when we both knew there were none. If nothing else, when the subject of the yips came up anywhere in the game, the first names put to them might very well have been in that little room: "Let's see, there was Blass . . . , and Ankiel . . . " Followed by expressions that moaned, "Those poor bastards."

He was a happy guy and a good storyteller. He laughed easily. I liked him. It was plain that four decades had eased the trauma of losing prime seasons to a defect no one understood, least of all him. A page at a time, the calendar had done its job for Steve. He'd been married to Karen for fifty-two years. They'd raised two boys. He'd remained near the game, in a city that adored him, scars and all.

Yet it won't ever let go. That's the ruthless truth of it, and if you're Steve Blass or, say, me, you may as well learn to live with that. For a period of our lives, we'd been pretty good at something. We were big-league pitchers. We knew that wouldn't last forever, but twenty-one years old or even thirty-one years old hardly seemed a time to stop believing in tomorrow. Our arms were strong. Our hearts were set to the rhythms of the game. So we'd run our laps and take the ball and try to throw it past hitters. That was the plan.

And there we were, five feet from each other, neither with a notion of what had brought us together. The symptoms showed the same, rendered a quarter of a century apart. The cause, though? Was there something in our brains? Something in our pasts? What had made us vulnerable, and allowed just about everyone else to look away and to go on pitching and playing?

What was it with us?

Steve shrugged. I shrugged.

He'd enjoyed a pleasant upbringing with attentive parents. He'd had meaningful relationships. He'd had his own family that he loved. They loved him back. The job was going great. My life had been slightly more complicated, but until that afternoon on that mound in St. Louis, I'd had no idea what an anxiety attack was, and even then it took months to recognize it for what it was. Point is, while our backgrounds differed, Steve had thought life was going pretty well. So had I, if in a somewhat different way. He ended up making a professional start drunk on a bottle of wine. That was the difference between us. I chose vodka.

"I remember sitting in my backyard at 4 in the morning, tears coming down my face, asking, 'Why?'" Steve said. "Because I didn't know what caused it. To this day I don't know why."

His expression changed from lively to hard. I wondered if he was feeling what I was, the slight turn of the stomach, the subtle disorientation that reminded me I could conjure the panic whenever I wanted. Put me on a mound in my imagination, put a ball in my hand, ask me to throw a strike . . .

"The most god-awful thing," Steve continued, "is being in front of thirty thousand people when you know you shouldn't be out there. I couldn't make myself quit, and I threw from behind the mound, I threw on my

knees, I threw halfway from the mound. I was in the bullpen when I knew I wasn't going to be used, and I would
throw every pitch for both pitchers; I'd throw 250 pitches
just to see if I could force myself. It was just awful. Then,
going to the minor leagues, by then, I was a cartoon."

We were strangers held together by baseball, an ability to play it for a period of time and two slow, terrible,
humiliating divorces from it. I saved the relationship
with a bat and a glove. Steve sat behind a microphone and
found some peace in the crowds and games that would
grow before him most nights. Years later, he old and gray,
I wondering what was next, we smothered our old frus-
trations in laughs that were mostly genuine and in sighs
that were fully so. He'd made the best of a time in his life
that hadn't gone anything like he'd expected or wanted.
He'd raised those boys of his, the boys who at a young
age would come home with autograph requests from their
classmates, who'd later come home asking why those same
classmates were calling their father a bum. They got over
that, just as Steve had, and Karen had. If anything, Pirates fans felt deep sympathy for their World Series hero
turned emotional wreck, even if they didn't quite understand it. They missed Steve Blass, though probably not
nearly as much as he missed them.

He would take some comfort, even forty years later, in
having tried every available remedy, no matter how hopeless it seemed. By the time he walked off a spring training
field in Bradenton, Florida, his head down and his sons'
hands in his, he'd attempted hypnosis and meditation
and overthrowing and not throwing. He'd tried pitching

drunk. As his career spiraled, bringing with it a good part of his life, the single bit of clarity was that he couldn't look up at eighty-five years old and wish he'd done more. There'd already been enough regret.

"If I'd have known then what's going on now," he said, "I would have taken myself to Harvard Medical School and said, 'Here I am, boys. Fix it.' But we didn't have that then, that sports psychology."

What they had was a corner bar, and a lot of lonely drives home, and twenty-four teammates who hadn't the slightest idea of what to say to help. Well, we have sports psychologists now, and we still have all the other stuff too, and hardly any more answers. The nightmares still come. People still ask, total strangers, as if they were musing on a coming rainstorm.

Hey, what happened? How come you fell apart like that? That musta been terrible, huh, Steve? Ever figure that out? Woo-wee, you were awful, huh?

"It's too personal," he said.

"None of their business," I offered.

He shook his head.

"None of their business," he repeated.

"They don't know you well enough," I said.

"You can't say, 'Hello, it's nice to meet you, what went wrong?' I want to slap their face."

"That's when I say, 'You don't know me well enough to ask that question.'"

Steve tried to tell himself then, and still tells himself now, "It's what you do, not who you are."

It's true. But try telling that to a twenty-one-year-old who sees only baseball ahead, or even a thirty-two-year-old who sees only baseball when he looks back. Try walking down the street and having every set of eyes remind you of it.

He stood in that little room with the humming refrigerator, and he gave me a long hug. I think, even after so many decades, he needed it more than I did. He smiled and said to call anytime. I told him I would.

He was right, I thought. Nobody knows like we do. Nobody. Lucky for them.

CHAPTER
THIRTEEN

Gary Bennett Jr. was a professional catcher for nineteen years. He could throw a baseball sixty feet without the slightest anxiety for seventeen of them. The last two he drank himself to sleep most nights and prayed he would not be in the lineup the next day.

He retired at thirty-six because of the yips.

In the spring of 2015, Gary was in St. Louis for the Cardinals' fantasy camp. He'd played for the Cardinals for two seasons: in 2006, when they beat the Detroit Tigers in the World Series, and in 2007, when he made one odd throw in spring training and never again felt right with a baseball in his hand.

Gary was not one of the great Cardinals, but he was a good-enough one, and certainly one of the better guys.

We were teammates for about two months in 2007, from the day in August when I became a major-league out-fielder to the day the season ended and he could go home to not think about baseball for a few months.

We'd seen each other occasionally since, usually at events such as the fantasy camp. I'd asked him for some time to talk about the phenomenon we shared, though we both knew it was optimistic to express it in the past tense. That little guy still sat on our shoulders, daring us to try a throw, even in fantasy camp. We met on a Wednesday evening in the lobby of the Westin Hotel, a block from Busch Stadium. The Cardinals played the Milwaukee Brewers that afternoon. I brought a bucket of Bud Lights from the bar. He sat down, easygoing as always, and drew a dripping bottle from the ice.

"It was spring training, 2007," he said. "The bases were loaded. Jason Isringhausen's on the mound. I went to throw the ball back; I just held on to it too long. I, like, stiffened up and I bounced it and he ran off the mound and had to grab it. And then, the next pitch, all I could think of was *All right, take your arm back*, and everything got real stiff and real mechanical from that point on. After, I'm like, *What the hell?* It affected me. It got worse in '08. It got considerably worse in '08."

Gary managed a smile. What's done is done. Right?

He'd caught fourteen games after I'd been called up in 2007. I'd not known he had the Thing. He'd covered it well enough, or I'd refused to see it. Nobody'd talked about it. I was in the big leagues, I'd spent so many years pushing the yips out of my head, and things were going so well, it had simply not registered that the guy three hundred feet away might be in distress.

He smiled again with some weariness and emptied his beer.

"All of a sudden," he said, "I didn't know how to put one foot in front of the other. I didn't know how to inhale or exhale. That's what was crazy to me, was, you know, since I can barely remember, four years old, I can pick up this ball and throw it at some semblance of an area, and now I can't throw it fifty-eight or sixty feet, or wherever the pitcher was. Within a wingspan? Six feet? Five feet?"

The shortest distances were the hardest, I said. In the worst of it, he'd had the pitcher come down off the mound into the grass, a few steps closer, and closer still. Gary would work up the courage to flip the ball toward him in a soft, pathetic-feeling, wounded arc designed for damage control. He might have had to do this more than a hundred times a game, throwing against the tension in his fingers, his hand, his wrist, his elbow, up to his shoulder, but mostly in his head. In his subconscious, he didn't mind when a batter put a ball in play—it'd be one fewer throw back to the pitcher. On foul balls, he'd ask the umpires to throw in the new balls. Jim Joyce, the veteran umpire who'd seen it all, was especially accommodating. It was humiliating, but not worse than two-hopping a toss to the pitcher or, hell, on the really bad days, four-hopping the shortstop.

His body had turned on him. The game too. I knew the feeling. I knew the pain would not be confined to three hours. I knew there were ways to cope with the twenty-one hours around those, and they weren't always healthy.

Gary held up the fresh Bud Light in his hand. His therapy. His friend.

"I'd have drinks, and I'd find a movie that would take my mind off it," he said. "Then I would sleep as long as I could possibly sleep, get up at 2 and go to the park, so I wouldn't have to think about it. If I got up too early, at 7:30 or 8 or whatever, I'd get breakfast, set my alarm for 2, and go right back to sleep. Then as soon as my eyes opened . . .

"I don't know what the definition of clinically depressed is, but during that '08 season, I was. All I wanted to do was have a beer or sleep. That's all I wanted. And this helped me not think about it. When I was sleeping, if I dreamed about it, fine, but I was still sleeping, or I'd think other things. Last thing I wanted to do was pull it apart, examine it."

Gary's baseball life became absurd, because that's where the monster dragged all of us just before it swallowed up the rest of our lives, made those absurd too. He was a catcher who didn't want to catch, a ballplayer who was afraid to play ball, a man who didn't know where to go for answers beyond a bar and a hotel room with blackout curtains. The problems of our adulthood had always been soothed before—or perhaps put off—by the hours at the ballpark. If he could've, Gary said, he would have lived there, because it was about his favorite place in the world. Until it wasn't, and it had turned on him just as it had the rest of us, and then he could barely hold up under the thought of it.

Gary was born and raised in Waukegan, Illinois, about an hour's drive north from Wrigley Field. His father was a welder and a roofer who turned the television channel to the ball game—Cubs or White Sox—every night. Among the first photographs of Gary and his father is one of the two playing catch. Gary is in a diaper.

He was a catcher almost from the get-go.

"I had a good, quick first step," he said, grinning. "After that, my range tapered off quickly."

So not just a catcher, a born catcher.

A month and a half after his eighteenth birthday, Gary was drafted in the eleventh round—293rd overall—by the Phillies. He turned them down. He would play college ball, and from a list of seven or eight possibilities, among them Indiana, Wisconsin, and Creighton, he chose Southwest Missouri State. When his father asked why Southwest Missouri State, Gary told him, "I think that's the best chance I'll have to compete for playing time."

His father nodded and gave Gary one of those let-me-get-this-straight looks.

"So," he said, "you're picking your college strictly on the baseball program and how much you'll play."

More a statement than a question. Gary nodded.

"Interesting," his father said.

Gary called the Phillies and signed.

Over thirteen seasons spread across eight teams, Gary batted .241, nursed more than a few pitchers through good starts and bad, and generally held down the games behind the starting catcher. He was tough and prepared and confident, what the men in the clubhouse would call "a gamer."

"I felt I got the most out of what I had," he said.

When you can look back on your days as a ballplayer and swear to yourself that you gave it everything you had, every day, every year, then that's a career. That's what the jerseys framed in Gary's den will remind him of. That's what the friends he takes into middle age will represent. That's what the backache and knee replacements will be for, and why he'd wobble around after games with concussion symptoms so severe he couldn't remember his wife's phone number; the privilege of that life and the respect he tried to pay it every single day.

It thanked him at the end by saying, "Strap in—there isn't enough beer in the world to save you."

Gary would at times test that theory. Anything that might pull him from the darkness, the fear of the darkness, was in play. That meant visualization. That meant thousands of dry throws, a balled-up pair of socks in his hand in a hotel room who knows where. It meant laughing at it, crying about it, hiding it, letting it out into the world, breathing in for four counts, holding it for five, releasing it for seven. It worked in the hotel room. And then his arm would seize anyway, as though it had been turned to stone, resisting a lifetime of ease and fluidity and muscle memory.

He was thirty-six when the 2008 season ended. By any measure, his body had baseball seasons left in it. He called his agent and said, "Don't try to find me a job."

"But Gary . . . "

"Just don't."

Seven years later, over a couple Bud Lights and a basket of wings, Gary said the nightmares were gone. There'd been an issue at his son's Little League game once—his ceremonial first pitch on opening day had hit the backstop with an embarrassing clunk—but real life doesn't involve a lot of sixty-foot throws. He can attend fantasy camps, catch up with old friends, and wrestle through a few throws—from third base—and make peace with the idea that not everything ends with solid contact and a victory parade. Sometimes things end with an ignored phone that wasn't going to ring much anyway.

He coped. He'd played all or parts of eleven big-league seasons before the Thing came for him, which is better than most. At least there was that. But looking that night at Gary, I could see that there was more under the stories we laughed at. Those baseballs he spiked, those throws he sailed into the right-field corner, those afternoons he spent wishing there weren't games those nights, a guy doesn't just retire from that. Guys like Gary, they don't walk away from a minute of baseball if they don't have to. He left two, maybe three, years early. That's a lot of baseball, a lot of life, unplayed and unlived.

In some ways, I told him, the Thing is not unlike cancer. A lot of people who get cancer did nothing to attract it. They are not flawed people. They did not abuse themselves. It's not as though they stood too close to someone who already had cancer. So they, perhaps, can wonder why they were chosen, but they cannot blame themselves.

"It's not your fault," I said, repeating a line I heard often.

Gary nodded and looked up. He tried not to overthink it anymore. He preferred to remember that championship season and, even smaller, so much of the good that came of his playing baseball. The feel of a handshake after a win. The flutter of two fingers calling for a curveball when the scouting report said never throw this guy a curveball, followed by strike three. The few minutes before a game when, hell, anything could happen, but the view was great and the anticipation was exhilarating. Where'd that go? Why'd that have to go?

The last time he stood on a baseball field, after all those wonderful years, he didn't want to be standing on a baseball field.

"It sucked," he said. "It absolutely sucked."

After a pause, he said, "It weighs on me that I ran from it."

He didn't run, I tried to remind him. He was taken away.

"I would like," Gary began, then restarted, "I'd want to know why. I would like to know why. Why the fuck did this happen. Not 'Why me?' but why does it happen to anybody? For so long you go from doing this, this, and this. You don't think about it. And all of a sudden you lose the ability to do that, and you have to think about it. Why? What changed?"

I couldn't answer him, so I just stared back.

"I care, actually," he said. "I would definitely want to know why. Not that it's going to change my life or the way I do anything, but it would just be nice to say, 'Oh, OK.'"

He just wanted to get it.

CHAPTER
FOURTEEN

I threw the pitch, which lowered the lever, which released the anxiety, like a cement mixer had emptied itself into my head.

There was the question, now that I'd been afflicted, of what to do with that. The immediate answer was to throw another pitch. (That would be the plan for what seemed a very, very long time.)

I didn't dare look into the dugout. Weak pitchers, insecure pitchers, they look into the dugout, their eyes begging to be saved: "Come. Get. Me. Hurry." I instead would compose myself, throw a strike, win this game, right now. Then another Braves hitter would step into the batter's box, maybe not dig in like he might otherwise, and I couldn't get it right. Like I was standing on someone else's legs. Throwing with someone else's arm. Thinking with someone else's brain.

And the ball would do what it wanted, not what I wanted. Like I'd lit its fuse and let it go and it would whistle and fly off in a cartoonish spiral.

Oh, shit, Tony La Russa thought.

Dave Duncan stood near La Russa. He searched my delivery for a glitch. *Nothing glaring,* he thought. *Nothing to explain this. The release point is wrong,* he thought, *but why? The rest of it looks fine.* He looked at La Russa. La Russa returned the gaze. Their eyes spoke: *Uh-oh.*

Get him through this, they thought. *Get him through this game, the next, get him through the winter, he'll come back fine. Hell, get him through a pitch. One normal pitch.*

Scott Boras watched on television from Newport Beach, California. He followed the flight of one pitch. Then another. And another. He picked up the phone and called Harvey Dorfman, the sports psychologist I'd met the previous spring.

"You watch?" he said.

"Yep," Harvey said.

"Something's up."

"I could see that, Scott."

"Maybe it's a blister. Could be a blister."

"That look like a blister to you?"

"No."

"Me neither."

"But it could be."

Years later, Scott would remind me I'd had an accident in the days before that start, throwing a tune-up bullpen session. In the last half-dozen or so pitches, it wasn't unusual to have a coach or catcher stand in the batter's box, without a bat, mimicking a hitter. Apparently I hit that guy with a pitch. I couldn't recall it. Could've happened, though. Probably it wasn't why, three days and three innings later, I couldn't have hit him if I'd aimed at him, but there was room for one more theory. Soon I'd be collecting theories and amateur psychologists and nickel cures, but first there were more wild pitches to throw.

Mike Matheny watched from the dugout through narrowed eyes. He was the first-string catcher. His right hand was wrapped in bandages, the reason he was in the dugout and not behind the plate. *This is bad*, he thought. *This is real bad*. And, he believed, it was his fault.

Eleven days before, Matheny had turned thirty. The mailman had delivered a small, rectangular box a couple days later, a birthday gift from his younger brother. Matheny was leaving the house for the ballpark, caught the mailman on his way out, accepted the box and, in a hurry, opened it and ended his season.

In the box, sheathed in leather, was a Bowie knife. He drew the knife into the afternoon sunlight, the gleaming blade long and sharp and decorated with etchings of deer. He was struck by the craftsmanship of the knife and the kindness of his brother, a construction worker who would have had to sacrifice for such a gift. He'd have to call him, thank him. His mind returning to the duties of the day— that is, getting to the ballpark on time—Matheny casually slid the knife into its leather casing. He felt a poke in his right hand. The blade had sliced through a seam in the sheath. He snatched his hand away, and then there was blood, a lot of blood, and it was dark red. There was something else: the ring finger on his right hand, the hand he threw a baseball with, would not bend.

As I launched pitches that seemed to have little regard for me or my feelings, Matheny considered that afternoon a week before, the timing of the mailman at his front door at the moment he opened it, the knife, a seemingly innocent wound that of course would heal, and then the drive to the emergency room with a ring finger standing at attention. He would get a stitch or two, cover it up with a small bandage, and be on the field the next day, he figured. He didn't need a ring finger to throw. Nobody would need to know of his carelessness.

At the hospital, a doctor peeled back the gauze that had kept Matheny from bleeding on his steering wheel.

"Not that big a deal," the doctor told him.

"Yeah," Matheny said. "But this."

He curled his hand into four-fifths of a fist.

"Oh," the doctor said. "You're in trouble. You're going to have to be in surgery within the next three hours or we're not going to be able to fish that tendon out and you're going to lose a finger."

That sounded bad.

Matheny called the Cardinals. A week and a half later, he watched Carlos Hernández do what he could to save me, the same Carlos Hernández whose back was so sore and tight it soon would require surgery, and what Matheny wanted to do was walk out from behind the plate and tip his mask back and say, "Don't worry about that. It was my fault. No big deal. Next pitch. Who cares? OK, now, this is what you and I are going to do. We're going to throw a fastball on the inner half and beat this guy, get our asses in the dugout."

Years later, sitting behind a desk as manager of the Cardinals, Matheny kneaded the scar left behind by a hurried surgery.

"You know, I was upset and, on a selfish note, I played on five or six losing teams and never had a chance to be in the postseason," he'd say. "That bothered me. It felt like I was letting my team down. But I never felt like I did when that started to happen. I completely blamed myself. The difference I could have made. That still bothers me whenever I see you. Because I think I could've helped you. Now, whether that's true or not it's impossible to tell."

But, he'd add, "I wore that real hard, real personal."

That wasn't on him, and I told him so. Hell, maybe he held it off as long as he could, maybe it was stalking me the whole time. He wouldn't have been able to catch me forever. One day I was going to have to stand out there on my own and recover from disaster on my own and live with the repercussions on my own. I was the guy holding the ball. I checked. It was in my hand.

My rookie season was over. It had ended with plenty of crisp, confident bullpen sessions scattered around eleven walks and nine wild pitches in four postseason innings. Put me on a mound, put a catcher behind the plate, and I would throw hard, precise fastballs. Add fifty thousand spectators and a working scoreboard and somewhere between starting my arm forward and releasing the ball

I'd black out, just for a split second, just long enough to throw a ball to the backstop. I consoled myself with the long off-season coming, knowing there'd be no pitches to throw tomorrow or the next day or next week. I consoled others with a practiced "I'm good. I'll be fine. See you in February. We'll get 'em then."

The Cardinals lost to the Mets in the National League Championship Series in five games. That two-man rotation we'd ended the regular season with—Darryl and me—had become one, though Andy Benes pitched well and beat the Mets in game three. Otherwise, we got beat pretty good, and that felt terrible. Not only did I carry the unknown of my arm into that winter but also my share of the responsibility for a good team packing up in mid-October, before its time.

The world was scary again. Adam Kennedy, my friend and former teammate, invited me to Southern California for the off-season. He'd been traded to the Angels in the Jim Edmonds deal.

Adam was a funny guy who liked to have a good time. He also had a lot of confidence in his ability. So we got along great. Within hours of first meeting each other— he had been drafted twentieth overall, fifty-two players ahead of me, in 1997, and we'd been teammates in the Carolina League in 1998 and again in Memphis with the Pacific Coast League in 1999—we'd debated which of us would reach the major leagues first.

We were in big-league camp together in the spring of 1998, just pups barely getting started, and during a morning meeting I looked over at him. He was staring at me. I turned away and, a minute later, too curious for my own good, I looked back, and there's this guy, still staring.

I thought, *What the* . . . , but went on with the day.

Next morning, we were sitting in the same seats, and halfway through the meeting I looked over. Sure enough, he was staring. Where I was from, you only did that to someone you were calling out. The meeting ended, and I went straight for him.

"Hey," I said, "what the fuck are you staring at?"

He said, "What?"

"I *said*, what the *fuck* are you staring at?"

"Dude," said the guy I'd learn was Adam Kennedy, "I love you."

"What?"

"I love you, dude. You're awesome. You can *play*."

He smiled all loopy, the way he still does. I laughed. From that moment, we were friends. How could we not be?

We'd actually met a few months earlier, only not so formally. In Instructional League, I pitched an intrasquad game. He stepped into the left-side batter's box, and I figured I'd amaze him with my blinding fastball on the outside corner. He whacked it down the left-field line, just foul. I threw another, this on the inside corner. He lined it down the right-field line, just foul. He was all over the fastball, like he knew where I was throwing it. So I'd just have to strike him out with my curveball. He grounded that through the middle, like he knew I was throwing that too.

I acted unimpressed. What I was thinking was *Who is this guy? And why can't I strike him out?*

From the weird "I love you" thing on, we got competitive. Adam reminded me whenever possible that he was the first-round draft pick, even though we both knew I'd slipped because teams knew Scott was going to make them pay me too much. But, technically, it was accurate. When the clubbies asked the team to sign a bat for a fan or a local politician or somebody, Adam would be sure to be there first. By the time I'd get to the bat, it would read, "Adam Kennedy, First Round Pick." Somewhere in the clubhouse he'd be sitting, smiling. So I'd sign, "Rick Ankiel, First One to the Big Leagues." To which Adam would respond, "No, that's going to be me too."

By then, in 1999, we were teammates on the Memphis Redbirds. In late summer, Adam was hitting .327. I had 119 strikeouts in 88 1/3 innings. We were close to the big leagues, and we knew it. The St. Louis papers were speculating on when we'd be called up, and Adam and I weren't unaware of it, and the truth was I was rooting for Adam as much as I was for myself. Still, what would be a few hours, right? He'd get over it.

On a day in late August, the Cardinals' farm director, Mike Jorgensen, was in the clubhouse when we arrived.

"Rick, Adam, both of you guys in the office," he said. "Now."

It was happening. We were going up. And I'd be first, I just knew it. Adam and I glanced at each other, stifled our smiles, and tried not to run into the office and trample Jorgensen.

"Here's the deal," Jorgensen said. "Both of you guys are going to the big leagues."

All right, I thought, *a tie*. I'd have to take a tie.

"Rick," he continued, "you've got a bullpen tomorrow. So you're going to stay back and throw that bullpen, then go up the day after. Adam you're leaving tomorrow."

Adam side-eyed me. I pretended not to notice.

He debuted on August 21 at Shea Stadium, starting at second base against the Mets. I showed up two days later, in Montreal. By then, I was too excited to mind.

Fourteen months later, we'd work out at Edison Field in Anaheim, where Adam's Angels played. We'd hang out near the beach, have a few beers, meet some girls, worry about tomorrow when it got there. Seemed like a good idea, and it was, as long as I kept the games of catch at a distance. Anything that felt like sixty feet, six inches caused my psyche and arm to seize. Therefore, I avoided it. Nobody in Newport Beach knew me. It was about as far from Fort Pierce as I could've gone without getting wet. No one would ask what happened.

Meanwhile, Scott Boras and Harvey Dorfman had regular dialogue about how to fix the scatter-armed kid who kept saying he'd be fine.

Scott suggested to Harvey that he call me. Harvey resisted.

"He has to come to me," he told Scott. "It doesn't work otherwise. I don't have the relationship with him."

So Harvey waited. And I played catch from 150 feet in Anaheim. And I walked around the problem, even as the nightmares came, and as two vodkas became three, then four. I'd smoke some pot, hoping it might slow my mind when it was racing, only to find myself overanalyzing everything I did.

Did I always open the door with my left hand? Did I always turn the knob clockwise? Is this new? Which hand did I hold the TV remote with? Have my car keys always been in my right pocket? Is this how I laced my shoes? One knot or two? Which hand did I brush my hair with yesterday? And I'd weigh the brush in my right hand, then my left, then the right again.

That was enough of the pot.

The strategy to calm my heart and mind was working. Not that I was ready to pitch. Not yet. But the distance was reassuring. The yips would require time to clear my system. This was my strategy. Ignore them. Run the stairs. Push the weights. Get a beer. Have a laugh with Adam. Watch the sun set. Think good thoughts. Try to sleep. Beat this thing. Start over.

Southern California was as good a place as any, better than most, and what I needed most in my life was quiet. I'd be fine. I'd be good. I'd see 'em all in February, good as new. I'd get 'em then. I settled in for a healing winter.

On the last day of November, a twenty-two-year-old man named Rob Harris argued with another man in Orlando, Florida. The details were unclear, beyond the belief they were headed somewhere together to buy drugs. They were in a car, driving through the city. Rob's girlfriend was at the wheel. Rob was in the passenger seat. The guy in the backseat shot and killed Rob, ending the argument. Rob's girlfriend got away. Hours later, the guy who shot Rob killed himself. Just a few paragraphs in the *Orlando*

Sentinel. Drug deal goes bad. Two dead. Life on the margins of a tough world.

Except Rob was a friend of mine. We'd played baseball together in high school. I liked Rob, and then he was gone because of drugs and guns and whatever comes with that. The phone rang, and when I put it down I began to pack for Florida. After a few terrible days that concluded with Rob's funeral, I went to my house in Jupiter, called Adam in Newport Beach, and asked him to send the rest of my stuff. I wouldn't be returning. I was home, and I could no longer hide in Southern California. I picked up a baseball and my glove, went into the backyard, and faced the cinder-block wall that separated my property from the neighbor's. On that wall, I picked out a nick in the concrete, a tiny flaw, one I could see from maybe thirty feet away. I threw the baseball at that chip.

Thunk.

I threw another.

Thunk.

Another.

Thunk.

"That you, Rick?"

The gentleman who lived next door.

"Yep."

"OK. Just checking."

Thunk.

Thunk.

Thunk.

Thunk.

The soundtrack of my winter. His too.

Right foot back . . .
Thunk.
Don't think.
Thunk.
Where was that release point?
Thunk.
I said, don't think.
Thunk.
Who cares?
Thunk.
Just let it go.
"Whoa! This your ball, Rick?"
"Yeah, thanks. Sorry."
"You'll get it."
"I know. Thanks."
Thunk.
Just me. A ball. The wall.
And the monster.
Thunk.
My mind fluttered away. To Rob, slumped in the front seat of that car. To Dennis, gone too, all those years ago. To Mom. And Dad, locked in some cell. I could hit the nick on that cinder-block wall. The concrete surrendered a dusty mist. The nick became a pock, and the pock rounded into the size of a baseball and grew. The baseball returned scarred on three or four hops across the lawn. The sweat soaked my shirt. I was hungry. But it wasn't quite right. It wasn't ever quite right. I'd take that fucking wall down.
Thunk.
"Harvey," I said. "It's Rick . . . Ankiel."

"Hi, Rick," he said.

"You wanna talk?"

"Do you?"

"Yeah, why not?"

Not completely committed.

"All right, then," he said.

Spring training was close. The cinder-block wall looked like I'd taken a pickax to it. I'd been through dozens of baseballs. My brain had begun to feel like one of those discarded balls. That is, together, still technically a ball, still anatomically a ball, but torn and out of round and not nearly as aerodynamic as it had once been.

In the four months since October 3, since the third inning, since that pitch went to the backstop and pulled the thread that sent me to the cinder-block wall, I'd tried to convince myself that I would will it away. Keep throwing. Keep sweating. Think it through. Bury it. Bury it under the memories of Mom and Dad and the shouting and screaming and humiliation and fear and regret. Bully it. You will not touch me. You can't. You are not good enough, or tough enough, whoever you are. Whatever you are. I will outwork you. I will not stop. I will win.

But, damn, my heart was running. My head was clogged. I closed my eyes and put myself on that mound in St. Louis, testing myself, and the crowd rose, and the moment arrived, and I was terrified. In my backyard, facing a wall, alone, the anxiety was bigger than I was. The ball was heavy. The air stuck in my throat. Spring training report day was out there, bearing down on me, and I didn't want to go. I couldn't. Not like this.

"Where are you, Rick?" Harvey said.

"I'm home. In Jupiter."

"All right. I'll see you Friday."

"OK, Harvey."

He parked in the driveway. I saw him pull up and met him at the door.

"Hi, Rick."

"Hey, man. How's it goin'?"

From that day forward, it was me and Harvey. And the wall. And whatever was beyond the wall.

Thunk.

Dr. Harvey Dorfman was a sports psychologist from back when there hardly were any sports psychologists, when it was easier—less embarrassing anyway—to just wobble to your hotel room every night and then sleep it off every morning. Many teams resisted the notion that a player's brain was at least as important as his brawn. Heck, most teams believed weight lifting was bad for a ballplayer—you were just supposed to stick to baseball and not worry about bulk. And now somebody wanted to get into their heads? Lots of people thought it was just stupid. Harvey had written books I hadn't read. He'd steered careers I hadn't followed. He'd soothed psyches of men—athletes and, inside there somewhere, men—I hadn't met. He was someone Scott trusted, and I could use someone to trust, as I'd run out of other ideas. If Harvey Dorfman could save me from myself, I could pitch. I could sleep. I could look forward to spring training, to the baseball, and to the people who would shout my name as I walked the streets of St. Louis, offering me a beer and a place to sit.

Harvey was born and raised in the Bronx. When the kids in the neighborhood were on the street playing stickball, Harvey was in his room, in bed, listening to baseball games on the radio, minding his mother and his asthma. Over the play-by-play of the New York Giants, he sometimes could hear the street games, and if I knew Harvey at all, he would turn the radio up.

Harvey grew stronger. He joined the games, played baseball in high school and soccer in college. He could see an athlete run or tackle or hit a ball over the fence. Everyone could. It wasn't enough for Harvey. He wanted to understand. What made the great great? What burdened the average?

It wasn't their strength. Or their speed. Or their coordination. It wasn't even their effort.

That appeared to leave one thing.

"You want a water or a beer or something?" I asked.

We sat in the living room.

"I'm fine," Harvey said. "You grew up near here, right?"

"Fort Pierce. Just up the road."

"Tell me about that," he said. "What was that like? Tell me about your parents. Your childhood."

I'd called him, after all, and I thought maybe that's where we were headed. And so I told him my story. The good parts. The bad parts. The frightening parts. I snuck up on the parts I'd never told anyone and hadn't thought I ever would. I liked Harvey right away, just as I had a year before, when we'd met. If this were going to fix me, then I'd start talking and stop when I ran out of courage or words, whichever came first.

Soon I wasn't feeling like a patient, like the off-kilter guy telling a near stranger his life story. Soon—maybe it was the way he listened, the questions he asked, hoping to understand—I wanted him to know what it had been like. How mad I was. How afraid I'd been. How it was I could be surrounded by noise, by people, and still be so alone.

For months, since I'd come home from California to bury another friend, I'd lived by myself in this house I'd always wanted. Yet I couldn't stop the internal chatter. It said I wasn't going to be OK. It ordered me into the backyard to face the wall, to throw until it felt right again. The day was coming when I'd have to put on the uniform and stand on the mound, when Tony La Russa and Dave Duncan would fold their arms and learn how the winter had gone, when Mike Matheny would gear up and sit on his haunches and pound his mitt and say, "All right, Ank, let's go."

C'mon, Rick, throw the ball.

That was the thing, really. Just pick up the ball and throw it. Except I couldn't. And I knew I couldn't. And Harvey knew I couldn't. And everybody standing there—Tony La Russa and Dave Duncan and Mike Matheny and every damned reporter—knew I couldn't either. I could hit that nick in the wall a thousand times in a row, long as I was out there alone next to a couple empty bottles of Bud Light. Long as my mom was safe and my dad was doing time and the only light was a pink-orange sun that didn't care if I hit the wall or the bay.

My whole life I'd carried a shield, forged from the belief of who I thought I should be. What a man should be. That is, impenetrable. It's what I became as a ballplayer too. I followed the best arm plenty of people had ever seen, and if it wasn't the best, it was close enough, and that made me invincible. What was I without it? The only place that would have me unconditionally—a ballpark—looked me over and said, "Prove it. Try harder. Want it more. Suffer."

Thunk.

I wasn't impenetrable. I was transparent. Anybody with a passing interest, anybody in a Cardinals cap and the mildest curiosity, would see who I was, what I'd become. I couldn't have that. I'd earned the other life, the one I'd had before, the one with the great arm and the future that had caused grown men to whistle and say almost out loud, "Goddamn, would you look at that."

And I cried. Sitting in my own living room across from a man I'd met once before, who a couple hours earlier I didn't know whether to call Doctor or Mr. Dorfman or Harvey or what, the tears soaked my face and then my shirtsleeve trying to mop them up. Of the two of us, only Harvey had known they were coming.

"It's OK, Rick," he said. "You were never taught how to deal with this. Starting today, we're going to rebuild your foundation, if you want. We'll start pouring the cement today."

I nodded OK. I just wanted to throw a ball straight. I wanted people to like me, to think I was a decent person, to forgive me for hiding from the person who'd hurt my own mother. For not smashing a Louisville Slugger over my dad's head and being done with it. I wanted Harvey, this man whose job it was to save Scott's clients from themselves, to like me, which was strangest of all. I mean, I barely knew the guy. And as I sat on the end of my couch, crowded into the corner against all I'd revealed, it occurred to me I might not throw a ball straight that day. Or maybe the next. It occurred to me that I wasn't merely a lunchtime session for Harvey. He hadn't come all that way to shake my hand and tell me I was going to be fine, that he'd fixed plenty like me, that all I had to do was believe.

No, I was a full-time project. Starting right then.

CHAPTER
FIFTEEN

I wanted to feel better about myself. I wanted to feel good about tomorrow. At the same time, I didn't want to care so much. I didn't want to carry a few lousy hours at the ballpark around with me all the time. Baseball had always made me feel special, and then, starting one afternoon, I didn't ever want to think about it. Before, baseball was the light that drew me through the day, that pulled me out of bed in the morning and sang me to sleep. Now it haunted me. Taunted me.

I needed a break, and yet the routine was relentless. Every day was filled with baseball, which meant failure, or the brink of failure, or the recovery from failure. Even on the good days, and there were good days, there was no avoiding tomorrow, which I tried to assume the best of. I suspected the worst.

There were ways I could have coped. I could talk to Harvey. I could practice distraction, optimism, and focus. I could count my breaths and ask my heart to settle. I could go to the ballpark every single day and work, and throw, and believe, until I was physically and emotionally spent. I could smoke dope and drop ecstasy. I could drink beer and pretend I was fine until closing time.

Because I was desperate to win my career back and be a reasonable human being and forget what an effort it was, I chose all of it. I ran every lap. I showed up for every drill. I threw every bullpen. I read every self-help book, including Harvey's. I'd never read a book before, not front to back, not even in school. Harvey handed me a copy of *All the Pretty Horses* by Cormac McCarthy, his go-to introduction to himself and the world as we would try to bear it together. Years later, I learned this was the book he'd first prescribed for Jim Abbott, another pitcher with challenges, and others he'd helped. By the third page, having read the first two begrudgingly, my mind lit up. It hadn't occurred to me that there would be books I would enjoy, that I'd learn from, that would offer a moment away from the noise. That experience—not only did I read every word, cover to cover, but I was sad it had to end—led me into bookstores, to James Patterson, to Dan Brown, to Lee Child, and then to the shelves where the books assured me I could be OK. They taught me the breathing exercises. They had names for the stuff that filled my head and quickened my pulse. They talked about the fear. I'd never heard anyone talk about fear. Not anyone I'd ever respected, anyway. A baseball field was no place for fear. Neither was Fort Pierce.

So Harvey would call every day. Or I'd call him. And maybe there was a message in *All the Pretty Horses* for me—he wouldn't really say—and maybe the message was that there was no message. Not everything had to mean something. Or maybe what was important was for us to talk about the two boys who'd up and gone to Mexico, which was when all the shooting started, and it's when our heads are low and pistols are hot that we figure out what's important. Maybe the horses are pretty, and they are, but that leaves an awful lot that's not.

By then, I was becoming skilled at looking for ways to escape. Some worked. Ecstasy worked for a while. Connections from home delivered it in bags or bottles, enough for a couple weeks, and an hour before meeting friends for a beer I'd swallow a pill. My heart rate would settle. I could smile and mean it. Laugh without thinking halfway in, "Yeah, but tomorrow you gotta throw." This, at twenty-one years old, from a place where drugs weren't uncommon, where drugs solved the smaller problems in the moments before the bigger ones arose, was my eject button. Get out just ahead of the nastiness, because the alternative was to stand chest-deep in the thought that I was done. At twenty-one. Having thrown 212 big-league innings. And the only place I had to go was home. That $2.5 million, minus taxes and fees and what I'd been living on, wasn't going to last forever either. No, I had one way back in, and that was to solve this thing, and that meant throwing strikes, and that meant not thinking about it anymore, and that meant not caring so damn much every second of every day. So, yeah, ecstasy got me through some days when I was drowning in apprehension, and it was never supposed to be the permanent solution, which worked out perfectly when the Cardinals asked me to meet with a doctor one morning.

"Listen," the guy they told me was a doctor said, "word on the street is that you are doing ecstasy."

I death-stared him.

"You understand," he continued, "you need to protect your reputation. And we do too. And the organization's reputation. Are you OK? Do you need help? We have people who can help you."

I stood up and walked out, went home and dumped whatever pills were left, and called Harvey.

"Whatever it is you're searching for isn't real," he said.

It felt plenty real. It was so real I needed it to stop. Because I had to throw tomorrow. It seemed I always had to throw tomorrow. While I still believed I would beat the monster, that the books and the breathing and Harvey and my own will to be the toughest guy in the room would win, I also understood—for the first time, with Harvey's help—that this was not going to be won in a single pitch. That this was going to get ugly. *Hell*, I thought, *I've seen ugly. Let's go.* I maybe shouldn't have been quite so eager.

The spring of 2001 was the worst of it. My days began in the dark, because I started long before anyone else at the spring-training complex in Jupiter. The events of the previous October had turned me into a national curiosity, which brought reporters and camera crews and questions and distraction. So I threw when no one was around, just as the sun was coming up. Dave Duncan, some unlucky bullpen catcher, and I would get to the clubhouse early, and we'd pile into a golf cart and putter out to a back field, where I'd stretch and warm up and then see what my arm had in store for me. It's not as though I hoped to keep it a secret. There was no secret to be kept. The hovering reporters, even the familiar ones who'd covered the Cardinals for years, heightened the stress in a fluid process. It was plenty hard when no one was watching. It was enough that I had to watch.

I tried to recall who I'd been only a year before, then a few spring innings from becoming a regular in the Cardinals' rotation, the start of a career—and a life—I had expected to be brilliant. Spring training had been fun. From teammates I figured to have for years, I'd made good friends. Darryl Kile had become someone I could talk to about pitching in the big leagues. Jim Edmonds was a veteran I admired for how easy he made the game look, a direct result of how hard he worked. He too had become a friend.

I liked being a Cardinal. I liked being a big leaguer. I felt important, as if I'd discovered exactly what I was born for, exactly what I'd fought so desperately to become.

What had been so easy—show up, stretch a little, yuk it up with the boys, throw a thirty-pitch bullpen, field some comebackers, run a few laps, shower, go home—was instead a daily test of my emotional stability. Hours before, long before dawn, I'd have jumped awake amid tangled, damp sheets. Harvey had told me not to fight it. So at 2 or 3 or whenever my nightmare had reported for duty, I'd hoisted myself from bed and turned on a movie, or ridden my bike through the neighborhood, or gotten in some push-ups and sit-ups, or turned to a bookmarked page and started reading about why my heart was running so fast. I'd fallen asleep thinking I'd have to throw tomorrow and startled myself awake thinking I'd have to throw today, and if I'd found a little something the day before that seemed familiar, I'd go stand in front of that cinder-block wall to see if I could summon it again. If so, and the arm stroke felt reasonable and the ball felt cooperative, I wouldn't stop throwing. *Thunk. Thunk. Thunk.* The soundtrack to my neighbor's breakfast, poor guy. But there was no letting it go, the compulsion to chase the reassurance of a single pitch that went where it was supposed to go, the drug that was *OK, that was good. That was more like it.* If not, if the ball came off my fingers sideways and that needed to be corrected, I wouldn't stop throwing.

All that by the time I had to get into my car and drive to work and go through it all again, only in Cardinals colors and in front of who knew how many people.

The strategy was to pretend I wasn't a mess. First, throw until I could barely raise my arm, then smile and not let anybody in, other than Harvey. So from the time I slammed the car door behind me in the parking lot to the time I opened it again, no one would see me suffer. I would not mope in front of my locker. I would not throw my glove in disgust. I would not acknowledge frustration. Nor would I acknowledge the reporters who'd come to see me crack, who, having seen no signs of cracking (other than the pitches themselves), would then ask—roundabout—if I was about to crack. The trick was to keep moving.

Harvey's usual response to an obstacle was "So what are you going to do about it?" He didn't say that often to me. I'd been doing something about it since I could remember, and he understood that. When home and family were toxic, I pitched my way out. When they handed me the baseball for a playoff game at twenty-one, I took the baseball. When that baseball went squirrelly, I picked up another and threw that one. He knew, without asking, that I had no interest in picking over the dramas along the way, in learning why I'd been left for baseball dead. He simply set about becoming someone I could trust, and cry to, and brag to, and laugh with. If he were going to save my baseball career, I'd let him. If he were going to make me a better person, I'd let him do that too. I'd even help him.

He was honest. He asked that I look inward, away from baseball and mechanics and what I owed—or didn't owe—the Cardinals and my teammates. He asked what I owed to myself.

"What are you doing?" he'd say. "What do you want to change? What are you doing to change it?"

I'd start to answer, and Harvey would say, "Tell me tomorrow. Think about it, then tell me."

He talked a little like a ballplayer, which reflected his upbringing but also the years he'd spent in ballparks, in clubhouses, in bars, wherever a ballplayer might be. He swore in a gravelly voice and never seemed surprised by an answer to one of his questions, no matter where the words came from. When I'd fall into a revelation, where my head was or why I'd done what I'd done, Harvey would say, "Exactly, kid. Exactly." Like I was solving myself and becoming more prepared for whatever came next. Day by day, conversation by conversation, I began to see myself through Harvey's eyes, the way a man sees himself through his father's eyes.

As part of the fresh start, I wrote my father a letter. Seeing as I wasn't much for writing letters, Harvey helped. When Harvey had asked, "What do you want to change?" and told me to think about it a while, I'd returned with a list that was, basically, "I want to throw strikes. I want to be happy." When he had responded, "What are you doing about it?" I'd told him I was simplifying my life. I was eliminating anything that carried anxiety, best I could, so the focus would be baseball, getting my life and career back.

And he said, "What about your father?"

The phone calls from prison had become relentless. The effort I was giving to stay positive—"I'll be calm. I'll throw strikes. I'll get this right. Breathe."—was, on a scratchy telephone connection, washed away with "Why can't you throw strikes? I can fix this. Are you hurt? What is wrong? Your mechanics are all fucked up. Those coaches are messing you all up." Some of the calls were angry. Some were belligerent. Others were worse. It was better to ignore the calls, which I did plenty, but eventually I picked up and almost always regretted it.

"I can't listen to this," I'd say. "I gotta go."

"Ricky, dammit . . . "

But I'd hang up.

Harvey and I had spent many hours on that topic. I'd seen and heard too much for the relationship to be anything but unhealthy. He wasn't going to change anyway. He was all I had, though, and even at twenty-one I felt a little boy's commitment—responsibility, even—to being his son. Maybe I wanted to make him proud, still. Maybe I wanted to show him I could do it on my own while he sat in a cell and counted the days. I wouldn't need him.

What about my father?

"My father," I said to Harvey, "that doesn't help any of this."

He said, "You need to break off the relationship."

"I can do that?"

Harvey chuckled.

I sat at a desk, wrote, "Dad," indented the first paragraph, and proceeded to tell him I couldn't—wouldn't—talk to him anymore. That I had too much on my mind already. That I didn't need the stress, the criticism, the reminder that I was less than I'd wanted to be. That I couldn't—wouldn't—send him $500 every time he needed it to keep him in prison amenities. That this was my life, not his, and what I achieved would be mine, and what I screwed up would also be mine, and that none of it was his to share, or claim, or fix. Unmentioned was that I'd found someone better than him. A man whose sole interest in me was me. I signed the letter at the bottom of the page, folded it into an envelope, and mailed it. A week later, the phone rang. I let it go to voice mail. He was mad. He was hurt.

I changed my number.

It didn't solve the problem of spraying pitches all over the bullpen. It didn't keep me off the vodka. I still needed Xanax to fall asleep, or Tylenol PM, or both. I still awoke in terror. I still sat in my car some mornings that spring and debated turning the key, and still was happy some afternoons getting the hell out of that uniform.

I was mad, plenty.

But it was good to know someone got me. It was reassuring to know that that someone didn't feel sorry for me and wasn't thinking, *What the fuck?* . . . That was enough.

So on those mornings when it was just me and Dave Duncan and whatever catcher was lassoed into duty (and, often enough, dozens of reporters), I'd pat my hand with the rosin bag and see what today would bring. Sometimes it was OK. Other times not. And then I'd go home to the wall.

The story had been a curiosity, but somewhat contained, in the fall. There had been baseball games to play, which meant access limitations for reporters, and the larger story was the Cardinals winning a playoff game, or losing one, or winning a series, or, finally, being eliminated.

The headlines had been along the lines of "Cardinals Survive Ankiel's Wildness." The look-away version, "Maddux Sputters in Braves Loss." The more pointed, "Cardinals' Ankiel Wildest Pitcher in 110 Years." The homey, "Wild Outings Make Cards' Ankiel Laugh." The reassuring, "Cardinals Still Back Wild Lefty."

Spring training was far more casual. For the most part, reporters could go where they wanted when they wanted. They could be in the clubhouse for hours. They could stand on a back field at dawn. They could wait all day by the parking lot, knowing I'd have to come by eventually to get my car. So I was pretending to be fine, and my team-mates were pretending I was fine, and we both knew better, and so did the reporters, but I was not going to relive every throw from every day. When I recovered—and I was sure I would, still—it would be with a clear head. Selective amnesia. If the fastball were misbehaving that day, then I'd throw the hell out of the curveball, thus far reasonably functional. The goal was to stay in the moment, to wake up on Opening Day with some confidence and a place in the starting rotation, and to leave it that small. It was challeng-ing to be asked to describe all the pitches that had zipped past the catcher three hours before, or hadn't. It was trying to be asked to sum up the state of my head, my heart, my nerve, every day. Normal wasn't normal when it came with dozens of news cameras and wandering baseball writers and sound engineers and producers who, let's be honest, had a better story if only I'd whip one over the backstop.

Some days I would be normal, or get close to it. Some days I had no idea where the ball was going, the newer normal. Others, the ball was fairly obedient. That was the roller coaster, not just on the field but on the drive home and on my couch and over dinner and in my dreams. Those are the stories that draw far-reaching interest, particularly in spring training, when a column about the twenty-one-year-old phenom who'd lost his way would get a writer to dinner with plenty of time to spare. That, in the newspaper business, was known as a gimme. "Go check on the head case Ankiel. That's an easy one."

Spring became uneasy for everyone.

"Stop," I pleaded to the jostling cameramen. "I can't work on anything. Just stop."

"Get the fuck out of here," a teammate snapped. "We're just playing catch."

Then that, of course, became the story, how edgy Cardinals camp had become, because the Ankiel kid was still wild, still had those demons. It made everybody more grumpy than they had to be, and then I started thinking about that too.

Tony La Russa fumed.

"The media should not be part of this," he'd say. "It's prolonged and beat up and feasted on. I see guys drooling talking about this because it's good copy or some goddamned thing. Enough is enough.

"Nobody gives a damn about Rick Ankiel, his father, this embarrassment. We're not going to help anyone have fun with him, with this."

Tony and Dave Duncan cooked up ways to duck the media. It was why I threw at odd hours, or off schedule, or in places off limits to anyone but players and coaches.

"A zoo," Dave would grumble.

Tony also worried over the strain on my arm, particularly my elbow. Just the season before, he'd seen a pitcher whose mechanics were not classic but were natural. My arm action was smooth. My effort was easy. I hadn't had to strain to throw hard. In the throes of the yips, I changed.

My delivery became more violent. My arm angle changed. First up a few degrees, then down a few, then up again as I searched for a reliable release point. It depended on the day, really, and then on what happened the last pitch, and also the number of bail-out curveballs that were necessary. He was worried and had no idea how often I was throwing in the backyard, how much tension there was in front of the wall.

Tony didn't say much. He left the pitchers to the man we all called Dunc. He watched and leaned into any progress that came. He suspected the worst, however, and hated it.

"I'll just say this," Tony said years later. "My respect, esteem, affection for him go to that spring, because this guy fought it and fought it and fought it. He never blamed the pitching coach, the manager. He didn't blame the mound. Didn't blame the catcher. He stood up so strong, taking it all in, internalizing it, this son of a gun. It's pissing me off, because he could have used all that strength to be Sandy Koufax and Bob Gibson. I don't know if that's a good thing to say, but that's what his potential was. The way he handled it, I never saw him show weakness. He just handled it. And I knew it was killing him."

We didn't have that conversation then. He was right, though. It was killing me. The spring games arrived, and little had been solved: the fastball was moody, the curveball was a safety net, the results were a moving target. And I'd be damned if I wasn't making that team out of camp, if I wasn't going to keep throwing, if I wasn't going to find a way.

I have one very vivid memory of the final month of spring training. I was the starting pitcher that afternoon. The start went exceptionally poorly. Before the first pitch, standing on the mound, looking around, the ball in my hand, I could hear the blood draining from my head. It was coming. I could breathe all I wanted. I could count backward. Think positive thoughts. Didn't matter. I was standing on the tracks, fearful.

This is gonna be bad, I thought. *Right foot back . . .*

It was bad. Also, it was short.

Dunc met me at the top step.

"OK, Ank," he said. "You all right?"

I stopped in front of Dunc and looked him in the eye. My mouth opened. Nothing came out. Not a word. Not a sound. Not a sob. I'd lost my ability to throw a ball and, in that moment, the power to put it into context. Not even "Yeah, Dunc, I'll be fine. Get 'em next time." Not even "Hell if I know."

I shrugged at Dunc. He nodded and patted me on the shoulder. I sat on the bench, lowered my head, heard the game but didn't see it, and considered how I'd just suffered a full-blown panic attack. I checked my breathing, checked my heart. And it wasn't over yet.

Somehow I made the team out of camp. The Cardinals were trying to believe, so I would too. I'd be the fifth starter for the 2001 season, behind Darryl Kile, Andy Benes, Matt Morris, and Dustin Hermanson. My first start would be April 8 in Arizona, our sixth game.

I was scared to death.

CHAPTER
SIXTEEN

I made six major-league starts that season. One of them, the first, went pretty well, because I was drunk.

On a Sunday afternoon in Arizona against the Diamondbacks, I'd make my first real appearance since the previous fall. I'd had six months to prepare. Physically. Emotionally. I had Harvey on my side. I had my self-help books. I had all my little brain exercises, my breathing exercises, down. All that had to follow was for me to walk to the mound in a big, full ballpark, stand in front of those people and the television cameras and my teammates, bury the past, throw strikes, and start winning my career back. My life back.

I knew it wasn't going to work. For days leading to that start, I knew. The nightmares came every night. I stared at the television in a hotel room in Phoenix early Sunday morning, hours before a bus would take me to defeat. All that walking around with a smile on my face for the past seven weeks, throwing decently and hanging on that, throwing poorly and dismissing that, promising better, would be exposed that afternoon at Bank One Ballpark against a team that, in seven months, would beat the New York Yankees in the World Series. We'd fly to St. Louis after the game. I packed my suitcase, stuffed my books into a carry-on bag, and rolled it all to the curb in front of the hotel. The mood was light. After three losses to start the season, we'd won two in Arizona. Now we'd have to get past Randy Johnson, who'd won the second of what would be four consecutive Cy Young Awards the season before. He was the best pitcher in the game. Tall and left-handed, he'd overcome early-career wildness to become this beast of a pitcher. The irony wasn't lost on me. I was a beast of a pitcher trying to overcome early-career wildness myself, except Randy probably drove to the ballpark that morning confident about his chances and singing along to the radio. All I felt was dread. I felt the Thing.

The ballpark is enormous. What started as just a roof in the distance in a few minutes filled the bus window.

"One hundred," I said to myself. "Breathe."

"Ninety-nine. . . . Ninety-eight. . . . Ninety-seven."

"Breathe."

Inside, I tried to lose myself in the routine of game day. The scouting reports. The conversations with Dunc and Mike Matheny. The music inside the headphones. The nap that wouldn't come. Early games from the East

Coast on TV. The clock on the wall was relentless, bearing toward game time.

In the hour before I'd have to go out and prove to everyone that I was exactly the same pitcher who'd unraveled on those mounds in October, I grew desperate. Weeks before, over a beer with a buddy, he'd said, "Why not drink before you pitch?" I'd laughed, then admitted I was sometimes better against the wall with a beer in my hand. The alcohol, I don't know, maybe it quieted my head. Maybe I didn't care quite so much. I hadn't thought about it since. I'd not started a big-league game yet either. I had to fight.

And if I couldn't bury the monster, I would drown it.

"Hey," I said to Darryl Kile, "think you could get me a bottle of vodka?"

It was humiliating.

He returned with a full bottle. Something cheap. No judgment. I shrugged.

"Do what you gotta do, kid," he said. "I understand."

With everyone on the field stretching, and so in a clubhouse empty but for me and a couple very curious clubbies, I took a few long pulls, felt the warmth and reassurance as the alcohol seeped into my bloodstream, and poured the rest into a water bottle, which I carried with my glove and cap to the dugout. It wasn't about gaining an edge but softening the edge. I couldn't trust me. Nobody could. But I could trust a water bottle filled with vodka beside me on the bench. I could trust a good, hard buzz.

The Diamondbacks scored two runs in the first, both on a Matt Williams home run, but I didn't walk anyone. By the third inning, we were ahead, 4–2.

The ball was jumping out of my hand. I came off the mound exhilarated. I'd struck out Tony Womack and Reggie Sanders to end the second inning and Luis Gonzalez to start the third, then gotten mis-hit groundouts out of Matt Williams and Greg Colbrunn. Right through the heart of their order.

Holy shit, I thought. *I'm back. I'm fuckin' back!*

Randy Johnson wasn't as sharp as he could be. The problem was, I was starting to sober up. I'd walked two in the second inning and gotten out clean, then gone straight to the dugout and my water bottle. The monster was coming, and I fought it back with a few squirts of vodka, then a few more. I laughed at the absurdity of it and, while locked in a battle for my nerves, managed to have a good time playing baseball. I batted three times, all three against Johnson, fully aware that Johnson and his three-quarter delivery were not always safe for a sober, focused left-handed hitter, and here I was an unsober left-handed hitter. I did get a bunt down. And I did manage a walk. And I did score a run.

We won, 9–4. I threw one hundred pitches over five innings. I struck out eight Diamondbacks and walked three, then went straight to the clubhouse and brushed my teeth and gargled whatever greenish liquid I could find. I was 1–0. I'd found a way, and it wasn't the perfect way, but it would have to do for now. I slept hard on the flight back to St. Louis that night.

Six days later, the strategy hadn't changed for a Saturday-afternoon game against the Houston Astros— fastballs, curveballs, and vodka. Survival, man. The monster wouldn't fight fair, so neither would I. Protective of me, the Cardinals had me warm up inside, not in the bullpen, where everyone else warms up. Just like spring training, they'd hide the fragile me until there was no way around it. At some point I'd have to come out and pitch.

I went another five innings, not as strong as the last five. I walked five, gave up four runs. We lost. And as I sobered up in the clubhouse, I wondered if I could continue like this. I'd thrown off the monster for a hundred or so pitches, but I could feel it adapting to the new 80-proof game, hardening itself against the vodka. What would I do, drink more vodka? Two bottles next time? And after that? Was this sustainable?

"Do what you have to do, Ank," Harvey said, just like Darryl had said, maybe amused at the tactic and definitely concerned for the consequences. "Just know it's not real."

That word again—*real*. Whose real? Mine? The box score's? The Cardinals'? My career's? Real was in the newspaper the next morning. Did you win or lose? Those nightmares seemed real. They were real enough for me. The sight of Mike Matheny pulling off his mask and racing to the backstop, that was real. Zero wild pitches in Houston. One back in St. Louis. Was that fantasy?

"Real," I told Harvey, "and the rest of it is getting a little blurry right now. I have to pitch. This is how I can."

"Ank," he said, "it's still there. You're not winning. You're stalling."

Damn if Harvey wasn't always right. My next start was in Houston. I had six days to prepare. I reminded myself it was me who had beaten the Diamondbacks. Me who'd survived October, and a winter of doubt, and a torturous spring training to outpitch the great Randy Johnson. My stuff had gotten those hitters out. Even in the next start, between the five walks, I'd struck out six Astros. The pitcher was in me still.

"OK, Harvey. I'll try. I'll try again."

This time in Houston, I went in alone. No bottle. No secrets. No pending hangover. Just me and the monster and the Astros.

I got clobbered. Over three innings, there were five walks. I hit two batters. And I all but gave up on my fastball, which had become too unpredictable, even by my new standards. If I threw seventy-five pitches, I'd guess fifty-five of them were curveballs. I was lost again. Totally, miserably lost. Defenseless.

When the game was over, I was waiting for Tony La Russa in his office behind the dugout at Enron Field. I'd had a couple beers. Tony had tried to push me back into the fourth inning. The first guy singled. The next guy, Craig Biggio, I hit. That was enough. For two hours I sat near my locker and listened to the Astros keep scoring. The cheering hardly stopped. By the time La Russa had come to get me in the fourth, I was down to one pitch I had any faith in. He'd said something encouraging as we waited for a relief pitcher to come in from the bullpen. So had Mike. The roar in my head drowned them out. I could see their mouths moving and feel the pats on my back as I turned to leave.

A beer in my hand, defeated, I sat on the floor in Tony's office. Reporters would soon be allowed into the clubhouse, and I needed to talk to Tony first. I wiped away tears, but they wouldn't stop.

"You all right?" he said.

"I can't do this anymore," I told him for the first time. "You've got to send me down. My arm is going to blow out. I don't know where my fastball's going, and I can't throw all those curveballs. It's embarrassing. I need to go down and work on it."

"Listen," he said, "are you going to be OK?"

"I'm going to be fine. I just need to get out of here."

"Go home," he said, "and think about it and tell me how you feel in the morning."

"All right," I said.

Home was a hotel room in Houston. Just me, a king-sized bed, a TV, and the new real. And a phone next to the bed.

"Why do you think this happened?" Harvey asked.

"I don't care why, Harvey," I said. "I just want to fix it. Just give me the steps. One, two, three, four, five, six. I can fix it."

"It's not your fault, remember," he said.

Harvey said that a lot. When he sensed I was beaten, or mostly beaten, he got off the baseball and into life. Real life. I was alone in a hotel room, which was fine with me, being away from friends who by their presence would remind me of the disaster I'd created of a baseball game. Harvey didn't like it, I could tell. I had a baseball career to salvage. He had a life—mine—to mend.

"I know, I know," I said.

"What are you going to do?"

"I don't know."

Harvey would have his two fingers of bourbon in the late afternoon, so I'd call then, usually just before batting practice, when I knew his day was about over and he was relaxed.

"You having your drink?"

"You know I am."

"A tough one last night, Harvey."

"Aw, I seen it. Be good to yourself."

"OK, Harv. You go easy on that bourbon."

"Heh-heh. I'm good, Ank. And, hey . . . "

"I know, I know. It's not my fault."

I was always going to beat it. Always. Somehow, some way, I wasn't going to quit, not ever. The drinking hadn't worked, so I'd done something else. Then that hadn't worked. I was running low on ideas. My confidence, what little remained, was shot. I stayed up all night, which solved the nightmare problem. *So*, I asked myself, *what now? Are you going to walk away? If you do, will you ever be back? You're really going to surrender?*

No. I wasn't. *You're going to drag your butt back in there tomorrow. You're going to run stadium steps. You're going to make yourself watch that horror film video. You're going to do what pitchers do to be better. You're going to outlast it.*

"Hey," I said, half in and half out of Tony's office, "you're right, I don't want to go down. I'll try."

Tony nodded.

"Good," he said.

I made three more starts—11 innings, 14 hits, 12 walks, an 8.18 ERA. I wasn't back. I was worse. The club sent me down to fix it, and I was relieved. More than three years passed before I returned.

CHAPTER
SEVENTEEN

Johnson City, Tennessee, population 60,000. Howard Johnson Field, capacity 3,800. Rookie ball.

A suitcase. A duffel bag. Some books. A serious crisis. Just dropped it all on the floor of a room at the Holiday Inn over on Springbrook Drive, a six-minute drive to a new pitcher's mound.

The instructions on my way out of St. Louis were something along the lines of "OK, Ank, go get right."

"I'll be back," I said, and meant it.

The first stop on my recovery had been Memphis, where the Triple-A team was. I made three starts. They went like this: 4 1/3 innings, 3 hits, 17 walks, 12 wild pitches, a 20.77 ERA. That's a lot to happen over 13 outs.

Somewhere amid the carnage, I'd walked the bases loaded, thrown a wild pitch, and watched from the mound as another run scored. A pitcher is expected to cover home plate in that situation. I did not. I'd not forgotten about that, and I'd not made the decision not to cover, exactly. It just happened, and I stood out there with my feet in cement, the blood draining from my head, unable to feel the ball, pretty much all hell breaking loose, and when I came to, the other team had one more run than I'd last checked. I wasn't trying to big-league anybody, certainly not my teammates, and I didn't intend to disrespect the game. Probably I was just tired of looking at stuff go bad.

I wasn't long for that game. The manager came to me afterward. "I know it's been hard on you," he said, "and I know you're frustrated, but you still gotta play the game."

"Yep," I said.

"And I gotta fine you a hundred bucks for not covering home," he said.

I looked up at him, by then half eaten by the monster, and was struck by the lack of compassion. Baseball rolls on. Baseball doesn't flinch. Baseball demands order. Pay your fine and move along. Didn't I know it.

"Whatever, man," I said.

The larger issue, of course, was what then? I couldn't throw strikes in the big leagues. I couldn't throw strikes in the minor leagues. The monster was getting bigger, stronger.

The club asked if I wanted to go home, to get away from it for a while. Scott Boras and I had a long conversation about it, and I talked it over with Harvey, and I told them all I would not run away. Besides, what would I be running to? A life in Fort Pierce without baseball. I'd had that once. I wasn't going back. What I needed was this, to keep throwing, to keep trying, to be around a game I loved even if it wasn't so sure about me anymore, to— OK—cover home when the game called for it. I should've covered home.

Send me down, I asked.

You're already down, they said.

Lower, I said.

The idea was to play ball again. Laugh again and mean it. To get out from under the lights, the pressure, the consequences of a bad pitch or ten. It would have been a restart, except I'd never been to rookie ball before, so technically the assignment was even more severe. The choice was here or home, and I wasn't going home.

Summer was coming, so the air was getting warm and sticky, like it does in Tennessee. The mountains were nearby. There was fresh water to fish on, and good music to go with the beer, and friendly people to talk to. The Holiday Inn was a star or two short of a big-league hotel, but it was plenty warm and dry enough for a guy down on his luck and looking to blend in.

I walked into the clubhouse at about the age a lot of guys walked into that clubhouse. I walked in with a grin, and my shoulders back, and embarrassed that I was there. Six months before, they'd all seen it. I was kicking ass, had left this minor-league stuff behind forever, and was up on that mound in St. Louis in the most important game that town had seen in years. Most of them would never see the big leagues, much less start a playoff game, and I had, and I'd retched all over myself. It was one thing to sense anger, even scorn or pity, on the streets of St. Louis, another to pull a locker next to a guy you knew was thinking, *Geez, dude, don't get any of that crazy shit on me.*

Rookie ball, man. In Tennessee. There were eighteen-year-olds on that team. One of them was named Yadier Molina. The future big leaguers were him and maybe one or two other guys. The former big leaguers? Just one that I counted.

The plan was to take away the top deck of the stadium. The second deck too. And the cameras. And the newspapermen. And SportsCenter. And a final score that would appear in any major newspaper. Just get back to a baseball and a batter. However many people wanted to show up, that was fine too, but they weren't important. Nobody looked at the standings. This ballpark, this roster, was about getting better, learning the game, trying not to be homesick, balancing a checkbook, saving enough money to eat at the end of the month, trying not to drink so much that you made a complete fool of yourself, even, for some, learning English and the ways of the culture. Me? This ballpark, this roster, this little town I hadn't heard of before Tuesday, was heaven. First thing that happened, I met the local beauty-pageant winner. We dated. She was nice. The next thing, they gave me a uniform and a day to pitch, and the whole thing was so delightfully charming I couldn't help but forget that a couple weeks before I'd needed a pint of vodka to convince myself just to walk to a pitcher's mound.

So I threw a ball off the backstop. So what? Tell that Molina kid to go get it. I'd wait. Go ahead, man, take another base, I'll strike out the next guy.

The plan worked. I pitched great, I played great. Again. In rookie ball, yes. Against a bunch of kids whose best stories were about high school. But still, great. A man's gotta restart somewhere.

Also, they let me hit. A couple days a week, in and around my starts and in-between-start throw days, I was the designated hitter. And damn if it didn't feel like high school ball again. Show up at the park, pitch one day, rake the next, laugh all day long. My first game with a bat in my hand, I hit two home runs. Say, tell me some of those high school stories of yours, partner.

From Harvey, I'd learned a technique—a game, really—that forced me to concentrate on something other than baseball and distracted me from the growing feeling of doom. Across a grid of ten-by-ten squares, I'd have a teammate write numbers randomly, one to one hundred, and then I'd search for the numbers in reverse order, drawing an X over them. Before long, guys were drawing them up without my asking, dropping two or three at a time in my locker. When they felt too easy, I'd listen to the radio at the same time, heightening the chances of my mind straying. Pitching well, even pitching poorly, was a lot of work.

Not to say I was cured or anything, but eight or nine months had passed since I'd felt good about myself as a ballplayer. I still had to practice my breathing, still had to settle into a peaceful place in the hours before a start, and was still haunted at night. But I also didn't have to pretend

I was fine when I wasn't. I could walk around between starts and not feel the weight of the last start *and* the next start. Batting practice cleared my head. Watching a game through a hitter's eyes again, measuring some young buck from Kentucky or California or Texas, remembering what it was like to have that fearless an arm and then learning what to do with it, then getting my hacks, the experience seemed to purify me. I could inhale and exhale normally instead of those tight little huffs that were all the Thing would allow. While I hadn't swung a bat this regularly in several years, the relaxation mechanisms that were hit-and-miss on a mound were quite reliable in a batter's box. The swing was rusty at first, but my mind was clear and my heart ran low. Rather than hoping to survive a game, I was competing for hits and for wins, and it looked and smelled and sounded like baseball again.

In 105 at bats, DHing twice a week, I hit .286 with 10 home runs and 7 doubles. In 14 starts, over 87 2/3 innings, I had a 2.05 ERA with 158 strikeouts, 18 walks, and only 8 wild pitches. Granted, it was rookie ball, and I didn't belong in rookie ball. But, given rookie ball, sentenced to rookie ball, what happened was what should've happened. I should've dominated, all things being equal, which they most certainly hadn't been. Any big-league pitcher would. Only, in the months leading to those results, those months thinking, *Oh, shit, it's my day to pitch. Oh, shit, oh, shit, oh, shit . . .* , there'd been more than a few occasions when I'd rather have been anywhere but on a baseball field. Also, if the rookie-ball thing had failed, the next level down was tending bar in Fort Pierce.

By late summer, I was looking forward to pitching. Almost as much as I was looking forward to my designated-hitter days. The assignment was temporary, and the plan was to rebuild my psyche and have a decent time doing it. The plan was working. Enough so, in the eyes of the organization, that toward the end of the season I was told the time had come to leave Johnson City and pitch at a higher level, in the minor-league playoffs.

I said no.

I couldn't stay in Johnson City forever. In fact, all anyone talked about was leaving, getting to the next level, inching toward the big leagues. Not me. Not yet. Winter was coming. I'd already spent one off-season troubled by the final pitches of a baseball season. I couldn't do another. The emotional foundation Harvey was helping me pour hadn't set, I knew, because even the mention of a bigger stadium, larger crowds, and playoff pressure stoked inside me all the same anxieties.

"I'm not ready," I said, that simple, and what I thought was *Is all the progress I've made really worth a playoff win—or loss—in Double A?*

Teams had come to Howard Johnson Field, and I could hear the young guys—the hitters—talking to each other when they found out I'd be pitching.

"Hey, can I borrow your catcher's gear?"

"On your toes, boys, this one doesn't know where it's going."

On and on . . .

And then I'd strike out a couple of them an inning. Decent fastballs. Not the 95 I'd had but a restrained, even cautious 90 or 91. Curveballs they'd never seen before and maybe wouldn't again. They were playing to make a career for themselves. I was pitching for my life over here. And I wasn't going to let anybody push me out of it. Not a pitching coach. Not a bunch of kids from down the road. And not the Cardinals.

No, I'd stay put, count backward from a hundred, hit another ball over the fence, strike out an eighteen-year-old and have myself a season I could be proud of.

The Cardinals couldn't have been too mad. In September, they asked if I wanted to come spend a month with the big club in St. Louis. I wouldn't pitch or even play at all. I wouldn't be on the roster. I'd come watch the games, be around the guys, and continue the healing from the dugout rail. For whatever reason, I'd held it together long enough for a few months to be not the pitcher I was, and not the untroubled young man I was, but a decent pitcher and a man who was surviving. That was enough progress for one summer.

In recognition of that progress, I may have celebrated too hard. Free from the mental gymnastics that got me to the mound, then kept me on the mound, then followed me from the mound, even in Johnson City, I had a good time in St. Louis not having to think about pitching. A lot of that good time was at the ballpark. Some of it was not.

In my apartment one night, I considered that the stress of the year—the anniversary of October 3 was near—and the various antidotes I'd chosen for it had found me in a reckless place. "Real" tasted better chased by Bud Lights. It slept better with Xanax. It looked better after one last round and a boozy promise that tomorrow would be happier. I was just trying to get through the day, probably afraid to face what everyone else suspected was true, that I might never be the guy who'd first gotten up on that mound last October. I was twenty-two. Nobody should have to think about that at twenty-two, and I wasn't about to, and the way that I was not going to was to remove myself from the truth of it. One beer at a time.

These are not habits that go unnoticed. The Cardinals gently suggested I go home, and I found myself agreeing, and I packed the truck and left. I'd still pitched all those innings. I'd still had a good time doing it. I'd played ball again, really played ball, and I was sure I was gaining on something better. Harvey and I would have the winter to get ready for spring training. I was optimistic. The dark thoughts weren't gone, but there were smudges of light that hadn't been there before. I'd go home and work on those.

Besides, that cinder-block wall was waiting on me.

CHAPTER
EIGHTEEN

There was more to the wall than arm angles and release points. The wall was therapeutic. The way some people meditate, I suppose, I went to the wall. People schedule their days around the gym, or lunch, or meetings, or fishing, or, say, a ball game, and I scheduled around the wall.

For four and a half months, in and around the rest of my life, from early October to the middle of February, I might not have missed a day. Sometimes that was twenty minutes on the wall. Others, it was hours, and I'd be startled to look up and see that the sun had gone down when just a couple throws ago it was midafternoon. It depended on the day before, or the pitch before. It depended on the ferocity of the night terrors early that morning.

At the wall, I was evading danger, an ocean liner zig-zagging away from a hostile submarine, just out of range. I was treating the fears that bad habits would stick or that better habits would fade, and those rendezvous with the wall smeared from one to the other, from day to day, from pitch to pitch. The wall fed my obsessiveness, settled my stomach, eased the dread that this was all leading to no-where, to a life in which, at twenty-two, I would be left to wonder, *What now?*

The sound of the ball striking those cinder blocks played to a rhythm that slowed my heart. *Thump-thump-thump. Thunk-thunk-thunk. Thump-thunk-thump-thunk-thump-thunk,* intertwined like that, finding a pace that soothed me into long breaths and slow, deliberate me-chanics, so I would not rush through points in the deliv-ery that were sticky and unnerving. Breathe and throw. Breathe and throw. Chase off the evil thoughts, welcome the sun and the breeze and the kid in the backyard just killing time.

"So whatta ya got today?" I'd sigh, and fish a ball from a bucket and go to work becoming the next Koufax again, or the first Ankiel, whichever came of that. Hours later, I'd lie in bed, exhausted, knowing I'd done all I could that day to whip the monster and fighting the urge to get up and throw a few more. Just a few more. Then I'd be fine. The Cardinals seemed to believe in me again. I seemed to believe in me again. So just those few more. I could make it even better. Those were my thoughts as I closed my eyes, of full ballparks and tied games and me with the ball in my hand again, everyone waiting to see what would come next, waiting to see if the kid had it in him anymore. And then I'd peel off the covers, pull on some shorts, pick up my glove, and go to the wall. Just a few more.

All of which, by mid-February, when it was time to report to spring training, left me with a very sore left elbow.

The magnetic resonance imaging showed a partial ligament tear. The wall had thrown back.

There are methods of recuperation from an elbow sprain. There are procedures to fix it, the most common of which is ulnar collateral ligament reconstruction surgery, known as Tommy John surgery. I figured I'd go ahead and get it done. I would turn twenty-three in midsummer. In a year I'd be right back in spring training with a fresh elbow. Maybe the surgery, followed by a year's recovery, starting over with a throwing program, would dampen the Thing. Most of all, however, my elbow hurt, and I didn't want it to hurt anymore, and I couldn't pitch with it like this, and I certainly was in no condition—physically or psychologically—to pitch around the pain. It had been hard enough in perfect health.

The team, in consultation with its doctor, outside doctors, Scott Boras, and, to some degree, me, chose a different remedy—rest. A year of rest. Go home, they said. Don't throw. We'll see you in December. Another summer gone.

I resisted. If something was broken, and it would seem my elbow qualified, the best option was to fix it. The worst scenario was to take a year off, in theory to allow my elbow to heal, and then return the following winter with the same problem. Then there'd be no option but surgery, and instead of sitting out one year, I'd lose two. Two more years of my prime. Two more years of distance between the pitcher I'd been and the pitcher I was trying to become again. The progress of the summer before would be lost to a plan that amounted to "Just rest."

The orders, instead, were to go home. So I went fishing. And I didn't throw. And then I fished some more. And I watched baseball on television and occasionally wondered if this wasn't getting away from me. And every once in a while, in the cool of the evening, I'd go to the wall, just out of curiosity, just out of boredom, and lob a baseball toward my future.

Darryl Kile died that summer. He was thirty-three years old. They found him in a hotel room in Chicago, hours after he'd been expected at the ballpark. Blocked arteries, they said. The memorial service was held at Busch Stadium in St. Louis. I sat with former teammates and future teammates and thousands of strangers, and I thought about Darryl's wife and children, and about my boyhood friend Dennis, and about Rob Harris, gunned down in Orlando, and how none of it seemed fair. Darryl had been good to me for no reason but to be good to me, and I wanted more than anything in that moment to be his teammate again. To be his friend again. I went back home, back to waiting on my arm and my career, heartbroken.

Nine months passed that way. My elbow still hurt.

I flew to Los Angeles in July of the next summer, 2003, days before my twenty-fourth birthday.

"Fuck this," I told Harvey. "Maybe I'm done."

It wasn't the first time I'd said it to him, but it may have been the first time the sentiment stayed with me after I hung up. I couldn't shake the Thing, the results on the mound hadn't changed, my elbow was killing me, and the organization now seemed to be losing interest. Through the frustration, through the pain, through the games, I couldn't see how anything was going to change for the better. If anything, my career was trending in the other direction. I'd focused for so long on the psychological element of who I was, fought that fight, and now my body was falling apart. I wasn't sure what that left.

"Then stop," Harvey said. "Write a book. There's your way out. Make yourself a little money and go. You know, Ank, there always are choices."

He said it as though he'd been waiting for this opening, for the frustration and embarrassment to become too acute to ignore. I was sitting on my couch and couldn't have hit the TV set with a baseball, for the aim and strength such a throw would require.

"I don't know, Harv," I said, maybe not ready yet after all. "Talk tomorrow, OK?"

I pitched fifty-four innings in Double-A Knoxville, Tennessee, that summer, and wound up with 49 walks and an ERA near 7. Since February I'd been buying Percocet by the drum, taking Percocet by the handful, to treat the pain in my elbow everyone seemed to believe was minor, or normal, or in my head. They had given me the ball and I had tried to pitch, and now the Thing and the elbow had joined up for twenty pitching appearances that had tested my pain threshold and my sanity. By June, I barely could brush my hair or turn a doorknob with my left hand. The plan hadn't worked, not even close, and so I was in L.A., and Dr. Lewis Yocum was threading out a ligament from my right wrist and making it into a new elbow.

I awoke from my Tommy John surgery wondering what I'd be doing for the next year, another one soon to be gone. I'd be twenty-five by the time I was on a mound again, going on four years since the pitch that had started all of this, and what I'd have to show for it was a lot of sleepless nights, a big-league ERA over 7, a terrific rookie-ball season, a scar on my elbow, and another on my wrist. On my way out, Dr. Yocum handed me a binder. In it, a manual on how I'd spend the coming year, from wrapping the bandaging in a plastic trash bag before showering all the way to ninety pitches on a mound at full tilt, with a lot of tiny steps in between.

Basically, I'd be learning how to throw again. And, well, that part didn't sound so bad. I'd also be learning to live again. Put one foot in front of the other, head down, a teardown and buildup, the way you'd—I don't know—pull all of your clothes from your dresser, refold every shirt, rematch every sock, and stack them neatly in their drawers. I quit drinking, a special point for Harvey, who for years had seen me hose down bad days with alcohol—and sometimes pills—and celebrate good days with the same.

"If you want to beat this, you've got to stop," he said many times.

I'd stop when the Thing stopped, though. It had picked this fight. I was defending myself, any way I knew how. Still losing, most nights, but still in there, still swinging.

I had the wall. I had my will. I had my books, telling me there was hope. I had Harvey by my side. Then I had my way of forgetting, if only for a few hours.

What was real? Everything but those few hours. The twenty-one hours around those few hours. The pain, the suffering, the fear and, yeah, the progress, the fastball that cut just a little and locked up a right-handed hitter to end an inning, that was all real. A little too real some days, granted. Most days. And still real. Still who I was, in there somewhere, in there fighting.

The beer, the vodka, whatever it was the night before, had taken to feeding the anxiety of the following day. The effort of holding firm against the Thing for those twenty-one hours, letting go for three, then returning to the emotional and physical struggle had accomplished little but leaving me vulnerable when it counted. I was still afraid. I would look into the stands and see strangers in football helmets and hard hats, mocking my inability to throw a ball where I wanted, laughing at the man who used to be Rick Ankiel, and I'd remember that only one person could throw this next pitch. I'd better find out who that person was. The way to do that, Harvey told me often, was to be that person—wholly that person. I'd run head-on into this for so long that the time had come to strip myself to nothing and know finally how it would end. No drugs, no liquor, no escape routes. Well, maybe the occasional beer. Harvey's point, that I must feel the pain in order to treat the pain, was that I'd require clarity to cope with whatever came next. To beat whatever came next. Or, perhaps, to live with whatever came next.

Thirteen months after Tommy John surgery, 1,399 days after October 3, 2000, I stood on a mound in Jupiter, Florida, the center of a Class-A ballpark called Roger Dean Stadium. Under the lights, after a day of rain, the place seemed cleaner, shinier, than usual. It smelled fresh, like all of the days before, the years before, had been washed away.

This, I knew, likely was my last shot. Maybe the Cardinals would stick with me for as long as it took. If not, maybe somebody else would take a chance. I wasn't pitching for that anymore so much as I was pitching to get it right. To win. To beat this thing and let tomorrow bring whatever tomorrow brought. The scouts could save the batteries in their radar guns, save the ink in their pens. I wasn't there for them. I was pitching for so much more. I was pitching for me, pitching for Harvey, pitching for the truth, pitching because the Thing had expected me to quit a long time ago. So I'd pitch just to piss it off.

I'd barely pitched in two years, and the innings I had thrown had been with a sore elbow. The recovery from Tommy John was arduous, physically successful, and in the end not a cure for the rest of me. From the first tentative postsurgical twenty-foot toss of a real baseball, I knew that I might have left my original ulnar collateral ligament behind, but not the Thing. It had survived. I returned to breathing exercises, to controlling the anxiety as best I could, even for those twenty-foot tosses. I watched games on television, studied the pitcher, and sought mechanical cures for my windup and release. For a year I inched along like that, the little guy on my shoulder reminding me my recovery would be his too, that he'd get stronger along with my elbow, and I'd nod and turn the page in Dr. Yocum's binder and find what the next inch would bring.

Those pages, those inches they prescribed, led to Roger Dean Stadium on August 2, 2004, a Monday night, the first batter St. Lucie Mets outfielder Lastings Milledge, the first pitch a ball, the fourth pitch rifled into right-center field for a triple.

"I'm still young, but I don't feel like it sometimes," I'd told an Associated Press reporter the day before. "I almost feel like I don't have time. But I do."

I kept throwing. Kept breathing. I pitched two innings, didn't walk a batter and struck out three, the last two on curveballs. God bless the curveball.

"He had such a sharp break on it," one of the St. Lucie guys said afterward, "you could hear the snap coming out of his fingers."

Could've been the scar tissue.

I threw thirty-three pitches, twenty strikes. I made another Class-A start five days later, another five days after that, and kept throwing strikes. Then two Double-A starts for the Tennessee Smokies, in which I walked two across nine innings, and a late-August start for the Triple-A Memphis Redbirds on a Sunday afternoon. The game was in Oklahoma City at Southwestern Bell Bricktown Park. I'd pitched there three and a half years before, days after I'd given up pitching drunk and begged to be sent down, and in three innings I'd walked six batters and thrown four wild pitches. I remembered there'd been a lot of football helmets and hard hats in the crowd that day.

Every ballpark could be a test of past failures and buried memories, some new way to summon the anxiety that was only too eager to return. The solution was to start at one hundred, work backward, breaths in between. Nothing had changed, except I'd gotten better at distracting myself from the catastrophe that could happen and chasing the outcomes I wanted to have happen. The balance was delicate. The effort was exhausting. And then it was time to pitch. In six innings, nearing the day the Cardinals would decide whom to call up for September duty, I struck out six Oklahoma City batters and walked none.

With a fastball that hung around 90 mph, which I dared not throw much harder for the effect it would have on my command, a curveball I never loved more, and a developing changeup, I'd made six minor-league rehabilitation starts on my new elbow. The results: 23 2/3 innings, 2 earned runs, 23 strikeouts, 2 walks.

August was nearly over. Three and a half years later, I'd pitched myself back into the big leagues.

CHAPTER
NINETEEN

I could pitch a little at the end. I could pitch enough to think of myself as a pitcher again.

I'd carry the approaching game in my head and my stammering heart all day, and in the hour before the first pitch, that quiet time when there was nothing to do but wait and think and stare at the clock, it would settle in my stomach. But I'd become pretty skilled at keeping the bad thoughts out, holding off what before had felt—and surely was—the inevitable wave of panic. In that way, I'd start stacking sandbags against it, counting backward from one hundred, inhaling between every number, and slowing my heart. By then, I'd rarely have to reach seventy-five or eighty before my body and psyche felt like mine again. The nightmares raged still. I had books to treat them, early-morning movies to soothe them, exercises to wear them out.

On September 7, 2004, after elbow surgery, after 101 2/3 innings in the minor leagues since the spring of 2001, after shutdowns and restarts and a good amount of tears and thousands of talks with Harvey and millions of pitches thrown (real and imagined), I walked out the front door of a hotel and crossed the street to Petco Park in San Diego. Jeff Suppan would start for the Cardinals against the Padres. I'd be in the bullpen for the kind of duty pitching coaches like to call "stress-free." For them, maybe.

I wasn't the pitcher I'd been once before. I wasn't the pitcher with the electric arm who'd pitched fearlessly from that unremarkable baseball field at Port St. Lucie High School into that soaring stadium in St. Louis. Neither was I the pitcher who followed, who doubted every foot-step, who doubted every arm stroke, who doubted every outcome—not really. I walked into Petco Park a survivor, still not entirely sure of myself but reasonably sure I could feel a baseball in my hand on a major-league mound. I would control my heart. I would see the mitt and believe the ball would find it. I would finish an inning having pulled my teammates three outs closer to a win.

So my fastball wasn't what it was. That was by choice. It was more reliable at 89 or 90, at less than full effort, than it would be at 95. My career, if there were to be one, would have to be about control. I'd control my mind, which would settle my heart, and control my effort, which would guide my fastball. It would have to be good enough. What others called stress-free I'd call being. Just being. Surviving.

The ballpark was only a few months old then, and in a way, so was I, at least in the parts of me that I'd been rebuilding. By then, I was less afraid. Not unafraid, and still capable of passing the security guard in the parking lot, carrying myself on sturdy legs through the hall to the security guard at the door to the clubhouse and finding my locker and the uniform hanging in it, all without my heartbeat running off. I was not twenty-one years old and untouchable. Not young, and still hopeful for the day and proud of what had gotten me to the day and willing to start over a different pitcher and a better, stronger man, now at twenty-five.

Frankly, it had been exhausting. And yet I arrived a relief pitcher with the other September call-ups to a team that hadn't seen much of me since, tears streaming down my face, I'd asked to be sent to the cover of the minor leagues.

It was a Tuesday, a night game in San Diego, where the air turned cool that time of year. These Cardinals would win 105 games, beat the Dodgers in the division series and the Astros in the National League Championship Series, and then get swept by the Boston Red Sox team few saw coming in the World Series. These were the MVP3 Cardinals of Albert Pujols, Scott Rolen, and Jim Edmonds, of four—Jeff Suppan, Chris Carpenter, Jason Marquis, and Matt Morris—fifteen-plus-game winners, of Jason Isringhausen at the back of the bullpen. And of me, a few years late and a few miles per hour short, for ten September innings likely meaningless—and surely forgotten—except for me.

Suppan pitched the first five innings. The phone in the bullpen rang. "Ank," I heard, so I removed my jacket, carried my glove to the mound, and began to loosen. The sixth inning was mine with a 4–2 lead. More than five years after my major-league debut, going on four since that playoff game against the Braves, an eternity in between, I loped across the field, kicked at the rubber atop the mound, steadied myself, and looked in at the catcher. It was Mike Matheny. Funny, I thought. Funny after all these years.

The first Padres hitter was Xavier Nady, an old friend and a good one. I exhaled. Matheny asked for a fastball. *OK, right foot back* . . .

Strike one.

All right, then.

Strike two.

Nady did bounce a single into center field. I looked at him at first base, like, *Thanks, pal,* and smiled. The rest of the inning—my inning—was as precise. Curveballs followed fastballs, and strikes followed strikes. By the end of a scoreless inning in what would be a 4–2 win, twelve of fifteen pitches were strikes. I'd had plenty of innings that had gone the other way.

Five days later in Los Angeles, I pitched again, an inning in relief of Chris Carpenter. I threw nineteen pitches, fourteen of which were strikes. So two innings, no runs, zero walks. When the anxiety bubbled, it didn't paralyze me. Pushing it away required time and energy, and the nightmares came nightly, and the remedies sometimes took more out of me than the innings did. As a starting pitcher I'd prepare to throw strikes once in five days. Out in the bullpen, life felt a little more complicated. I wasn't going to pitch every day, but that phone rings a lot, which gave me plenty of chances to breathe and count backward from one hundred.

A week after L.A., in front of more than forty thousand people at Busch Stadium, I threw two scoreless innings—nineteen strikes, eleven balls. I struck out the first three Diamondbacks hitters and later walked my first batter. It didn't bother me. I struck out the next guy.

The results were important. I'd take four innings over twelve days and a zero ERA, five strikeouts, and one walk. I got shellacked in Colorado after that, which can happen, and finished my season with four good innings against the Brewers in St. Louis. The Cardinals were going to the playoffs, and I was making arrangements to add some innings in Puerto Rico over the winter so I'd be closer to ready to pitch a full season in 2005.

More important, I could be in control. It wasn't easy. In fact, it was a burden. In order to be upright for three hours of baseball, I had to all but shut down for the other twenty-one hours. It meant little messing around with teammates and no time for—or commitment in—the rest of my life. I had to get to 7 o'clock, or whatever time it was when the bullpen phone rang, and the only way there was to drag my mind along a narrow, worn path.

It was work. And daily self-repair. From May 10, 2001, my previous big-league pitch, to my next on September 7, 2004, I'd searched and fallen and healed and wondered who I was, then who I'd ever be again. What I'd learned was that I could be a pitcher if I wanted it enough. If I was willing to sacrifice the rest of my life for it. Maybe I wouldn't be a great pitcher, maybe I would, but what became important was winning the game around the game, the one in my head.

The fight chose me. It would get a fight back. There was no other way. That was what September of 2004 was about—wearing a big-league uniform and standing on a big-league mound and getting big-league hitters out and feathering in the second and third decks, the television cameras, all the people, and a score in the paper that people cared about. I hadn't won, but I was back in the game.

I used to describe it this way: If a boy had reached to pet a large dog and that dog had bitten him, he'd think of that pain every time he put his hand near a dog again. That's what pitching had become for me, even when I was pitching well enough to keep pitching. Every time I picked up a baseball, I was reaching out to that dog. Its ears were back. It was growling. My heart raced. The blood drained from my head. I reached further and hoped it wouldn't bite and waited for the pain.

CHAPTER TWENTY

Four and a half years after the pitch, a pitch that even all that time later seemed so innocent, I retired. I'd taken the very long route to an afternoon on my couch, where I relived as much as I could recall if only to properly bury it.

I'd surrendered. And as I lay alone on a familiar couch in my living room, I thought again of those dark baseball seasons, the recurring nightmares on minor-league mounds and the restless nights in minor-league hotels, the major-league hope that was only that. They were behind me then, for the first time. I could have put myself back on those mounds, closed my eyes and felt the weight again, felt the liquid in my head begin to bubble, and felt the disappointment again. Instead, at twenty-five, I'd retired. My baseball career was over almost before it had started, and I was not at all unhappy about it.

I'd had to go before I turned into a roiling puddle of anxiety and was squeegeed into a drain and run out to sea, which wouldn't have been much of a life. One morning I'd quit my job and driven home and fallen into the sofa— brown, wide, and perfectly worn, as though I'd bought it all those years before for just that moment. I was done with baseball. Me with it, it with me, and now all I had ahead of me was . . . I hadn't the slightest idea.

Between my original signing bonus and the game checks I'd lived on for parts of four seasons at various levels, I had some money. Enough to take some time off and figure it out. Enough to keep my gas tank full, enough for a bucket of baitfish and a six-pack of Bud Light when I wanted them. That sounded good enough to me.

It was early March 2005. Four full baseball seasons had passed since my arm had deserted me. Another was in sight. I'd tried to be a pitcher again. I'd tried a million ways. I didn't have a million and one in me.

I'd been talking a lot with Harvey. More than usual. In my line of work, having a psychologist was viewed as a foundational weakness. My psychologist became one of my best friends and in many ways replaced the real father I despised and hoped never to see again.

I went to bed one night thinking I'd had enough of baseball. The next morning brought nothing in the way of regret. So I would go to my boss, shake his hand, and tell him. I was not going to be a superstar baseball player, an unfortunate outcome he likely suspected. I was not going to be a baseball player at all. I did not have a plan for the rest of my life. I did not have a plan for that afternoon.

The ritual that led to my resignation was rigid and comforting. I followed it that morning, though for the first time since before I could remember it would not lead to a day at the ballpark. Assuming I slept, which I probably didn't, I was in the kitchen at dawn. I liked dawn for the way I remembered it smelling, that being before the accident and the concussion, which jostled just enough in my head to kill my sense of smell. I was thirteen then, being towed on a skateboard behind a go-cart, an event that concluded predictably with a crash, a trip to the emergency room, and my being down one sense. Twelve years later, everything still smelled like the interior of a vacant warehouse, which, at the moment, sort of described my baseball career. I liked dawn because of its coolness, how it foretold—demanded, even—a fresh start, a ball's-stuck-in-the-tree do-over. Mostly, I liked dawn because it wasn't night, and so I wasn't staring at the ceiling or watching TV or reading a self-help book or listening to my breath while waiting for dawn. I'd spent a decent percentage of my young adulthood waiting for the rest of the world to get up, though I don't know why; I wasn't altogether eager to have the day start anyway.

From the kitchen I could not see the Loxahatchee River, but I knew it was there, and I could sense the snook coming to life. Snook season runs pretty close to baseball season, and I loved them both. While the baseball took me away from the snook, the snook were kind enough to reciprocate. At that point, I was in the business of finding places for my head to go. So I lingered on the snook, the carnivorous beast that swam in salt and brackish water, that hit the hook with authority, that ran hard, that wouldn't go easy, that wouldn't quit until it was hauled onto the boat and convinced to quit.

Then I'd go quit. I'd call it "retirement."

Egg whites spat at me from a frying pan. I poured molten bananas, strawberries, and oats from a blender, then thumbed my phone.

"Hi, Ank." Harvey was in North Carolina. He too was an early riser whose head was well into the day before the rest of him was.

"Today's the day," I said. "I'm going to do it."

"OK, Ank. You go do it. We'll talk later. You good?"

"I'm freakin' sexy. See ya."

I ate the breakfast that would get me through a morning of spring training, that on that day would instead get me through the drive across Jupiter, Florida, to Roger Dean Stadium, the walk to Tony La Russa's office, the walk back to the parking lot, and the drive home. The whole thing would take an hour, tops. My not-quite-eight-year professional career, from the second round of the 1997 draft to this—I wasn't quitting, I wasn't surrendering, I was retiring, dammit—would be gone in a thin smile and a promise to stay in touch. Nobody would try to talk me out of it, I knew.

The date was March 9. The day was Wednesday. Maybe, so far, the best day of my life. One of the better ones I could remember anyway. I'd pitched my way back to ten big-league innings the prior September in what I had assumed was a comeback. Yet as those innings faded, I began to understand them as something else. They were my opening to say good-bye. I could not leave the game in the middle of an inning, three runs in, base runners everywhere, my fastball haywire again. I could not leave because I was afraid to get on a mound. I wouldn't go out on an operating table and wouldn't use a fouled elbow as an excuse. I had to get back, to prove that I could, and if not as what everyone—myself included—had once expected of me, then something at least presentable. I'd leave when I was ready. I'd leave only after I'd proven it was possible.

For my last minutes as a ballplayer, I wore shorts, a T-shirt, and flip-flops. I backed the BMW, bought with ballplayer money, away from the house, bought with signing-bonus money. From the beach, past US-1, over the Indiantown Bridge, gauging the light, passing on the shortcut behind the Publix plaza, left on Alt A1A, right on Frederick Small Road, past Military Trail, through the roundabout, along the back fields of the baseball complex, right on University Boulevard, and into the players' lot. Country was on the radio. This was the routine readying for baseball. Hi to the security guy. A choice of doors: the one that led into the big-league clubhouse or the one that shot past the trainers' room and to the manager's office. The latter was preferable that day.

I'd been gathering the courage to do this, if not every minute of every day then often enough over the past few weeks. I cared what people thought of me. Ballplayers didn't walk away. They were shoved, forcibly removed from the premises at the end of a cattle prod, railing against the injustices of age and declining skills and the idiots who decided who was too old and unskilled. Real men stuck it out. Real ballplayers with nothing else to do were particularly obstinate. I could have kept pitching, stuck with the daily physical and psychological program that nudged me back toward the mound. In my heart, I believed I could pitch in the big leagues. I'd earned it. It was just so hard. It was just so burdensome. It was just time to stop, for those reasons. I was exhausted. So I was struck by the ease of the morning, the peacefulness that rode along with me and followed me toward my resignation and, out there somewhere, the rest of my life.

Tony La Russa was behind his desk. He wasn't surprised to see me. Most mornings I'd lean into his office and say some smart-ass thing, something to start the day and show him I was good to go and not an emotional wreck, and Tony would look up over his reading glasses and bark a response as I laughed and continued down the hall.

This time I entered the office and closed the door.

"What's up?" he said.

I sat across from him.

"I can't do it anymore."

Just like that. I can't. More, I won't. None of us could do it anymore. Not me. Not him. Not Dave Duncan, the pitching coach. Not Harvey. Not Scott Boras.

I. Can't. Do. It. Anymore.

Every word a hammer strike, loud and final. Each report echoing in my head as my old life vanished, my old dreams with it, dying of self-inflicted chaos. But now the words were free, sprung from a single pitch and the four years spent trying to take it back. My eyes were dry.

Little in baseball surprised Tony. If it did, he didn't much let on. The stone face, the sunglasses at night, the man carried himself like he'd seen it all. Probably because he had. He looked into my eyes for what seemed like a long time. This had blindsided him. I didn't have anything left to say and didn't fumble with an explanation. It was all too obvious.

"You sure?" he asked.

"I'm sure."

"Give it a day," he said, again.

He was concerned. I didn't want him to be concerned. He didn't really want me to give it a day. It was something to say when there was nothing to say.

"I don't need a day."

I hoped I wasn't disappointing him, but it wouldn't change anything if I were. We shook hands. I left through the same back door so there'd be no good-byes, other than a wave to the now curious security guard. Country back on the radio, left on University, past the back fields, the other way on the roundabout, past Military Trail, left on Frederick Small, right on Alt A1A, over the bridge, down US-1, to the beach, to my couch. Done.

They'd pack the stuff in my locker and dump it on my doorstep. I didn't have much use for gloves and spikes and old T-shirts anyway. The Cardinals would void my contract. There'd be an announcement of some sort, a press release, maybe I'd talk to the press. Maybe not. I'd disappear. Spring training would go on, and the season would come, but not for me, and all my friends would continue their careers, but not me. I lay down. The phone rang. It was Harvey. I was fine, I told him. Really fine, I said. Promise. I'm not depressed. I'm not cracking up. I'm fine. No, nobody's here with me. It'll be fine. I'm fine. Thanks, I said, for checking in, then set the phone on the coffee table.

I could breathe again. I could smile and mean it. That thing on my shoulders and in my neck, that heavy and dark and relentless burden that in four and a half years had grown with my ERA, it was gone. My head was clear. So clear, I had to laugh. By giving up what I'd thought was my life, I knew I'd gotten my life back. I knew it in that moment. I'd traded baseball for me. I'd miss it, sure. But it wasn't for me. Not anymore.

I didn't turn on the TV. I didn't turn on the radio. I sat on my old brown couch, happy to be happy, happy for the silence in my head, happy to be free, at twenty-five, of the only thing I had ever really wanted.

In Asheville, North Carolina, a phone rang, and Harvey picked up. Years later, Harvey recounted the conversation to me.

"Scott," he said.

"Well, he did it," Scott Boras said. "He told the Cardinals. He's not going back."

"I know," Harvey said.

"How's he seem to you?"

"He said he's fine."

"What do you think?"

"He said he's fine."

"I'll call Walt," Scott said, meaning Walt Jocketty, the Cardinals' general manager.

"You better be right," Harvey said.

"There's no more monster," Scott said. "We killed it. It's gone."

"All I'm saying is, this better work."

"It'll work."

"If it doesn't . . . "

"Harvey," Scott said, "trust me."

"Trust you? You kidding? You're more messed up than any of 'em."

Their usual dance. They shared a laugh. Maybe Scott needed Harvey more than I did, which was saying something.

"Gotta go, Harvey. I'll stay in touch."

They'd been plotting this for months. They'd had a plan for when I couldn't do it anymore. They'd hidden it from me.

I let my mind drift to the backyard games in Fort Pierce, Florida, to the early ball games at Sportsman's Park and then Port St. Lucie High School, the draft, a couple years in the minor leagues, my big-league debut for the Cardinals in Montreal a month after my twentieth birthday, my first home run, an opposite-field shot on a cold, damp night in St. Louis. The road to the major leagues had seemed wide and empty, without a speed limit. Damn, was that me back there? Had I ever been that fearless? That sure of myself?

Occasionally, as word spread that I'd gone home for good, my teammates—former teammates—would wake my phone with a text message.

"All good," I'd send back.

Yeah, all good.

"Good luck," they'd say.

"You too."

"We'll get a beer."

"Sounds good."

We probably wouldn't. I wasn't part of that anymore.

I closed my eyes again and considered the path to here, to a couch in Jupiter and a Wednesday morning in March with nothing to do but reassure those kind enough to reassure me. And to say good-bye. They'd go off to their lives, my former life, and I'd get on with mine, which at the moment had nothing to do with baseball and everything to do with a fluffy cushion under my head and, I didn't know, maybe some lunch or something. I could do whatever I wanted, and I'd never have to chase the fastball I'd once had, or stand in the middle of a ballpark in disgrace as my catcher spun and sprinted to the backstop, or fear my next pitch, or live up to the player I had been. I wouldn't have to be the guy who used to be Rick Ankiel anymore. Maybe I'd sleep again. The nightmares could go haunt some other poor schmuck.

On my couch, I was content. The poster on the living room wall behind me was from *Scarface*, one of my favorite movies. Al Pacino lazed in a huge bathtub, bubbles everywhere. He pulled on a cigar. In a lower corner, the words "Who do I trust? Me." I believed that again. It had been a while.

I'd just spent better than four years trying to trust everyone, anyone but the man on the couch. But I knew where my guy Tony Montana—Pacino's character—was coming from. I'd known that feeling once, forever ago. I'd been untouchable. They'd said I was gifted, that my arm was special. At twenty, I was certain of it too. More than certain. At twenty-one I stood on a pitcher's mound in a full stadium in game one of a playoff series, and from that height I could see the future everyone talked about, that I'd wished for myself. That I'd worked my ass off for.

From a slightly lower vantage point—my feet up, head back, eyes closed, late-morning sun on my face—I understood something similar. I was in control of my future again. So I wasn't going to be a special baseball player. I'd live up to practically no one's expectation of me. I probably wasn't going to be rich. There'd be no yacht, no mansion on the water, no easy life through middle age or for the next generation of Ankiels. There'd be no World Series game seven, me against some big ol' hairy dude, the crowd loud, the moment taut, me knowing I was born for the next pitch. Turned out, it was the next pitch that had run me off. I'd have to get a job, maybe go to school, sort out a life that had melted away on that mound and hadn't stopped bleeding until now. It all sounded so . . . wonderful.

In the beginning, when the monster was in its infancy, Dave Duncan had hope for me. A decent catch-and-throw catcher in the 1960s and '70s, he had become the most respected pitching coach in the game. Duncan turned out Cy Young Award winners and World Series champion pitching staffs, and he had a particular touch with pitchers who'd been successful but had somehow lost their way. He didn't say a lot, but the few words he chose were enough. His reputation was as a coach who'd turn rookies into men, average pitchers into good pitchers, good pitchers into great pitchers. The ones who came along great, he'd keep them great.

Then there was me. He tried. He knew pitching mechanics. He understood the mind of the ballplayer. And he could sort through an opposing lineup, pick it apart, and present the strategy that would work in a few simple, encouraging sentences.

None of which prepared him for the can't-miss prodigy who missed a lot. None of which prepared him for the monster.

"Dunc," La Russa said to him that day, "Rick went home. He's not coming back."

Duncan shook his head and blinked his sad eyes. He'd seen it coming and thought it was for the best. He'd been bothered by the previous four seasons, by his inability to fix me, to set it right. He'd lost sleep himself. He had a pitching staff to deliver by opening day, and there was plenty to do that morning, but he'd allow a few moments for regret. There'd been days along the way, moments, really, a pitch here or there, when Duncan had allowed himself a drop of optimism. But the next day would come and bring another bucket of reality, which inevitably got kicked over, drenching everybody's shoes again.

La Russa knew precisely what Duncan was thinking. They'd spent plenty of nights together considering ways to reconstruct me, and La Russa would wonder when the game might become fun again for me. He'd stand to the side and see me on a mound, watch me start my windup, and remember when he'd allowed himself to believe he was witnessing the next Bob Gibson, the left-handed version. *Wasn't that long ago,* he'd muse. He would not have said it aloud, not in public, where such reflections would stalk a ballplayer to his grave. But, hell, I'd had as live an arm as La Russa had ever seen. The way I threw a baseball, it was as if the ball itself was alive and couldn't wait to be excused from its temporary place in my hand. From the Rawlings factory, to the box with eleven other balls in it, to the ball bag, to the baseball glove, and then to my hand. These were merely transitional areas for a baseball on the nights I went out there and, a pitch at a time, tried to become something great.

They'd talked themselves out on the subject of me, and so in the brief silence between the manager and his pitching coach in the immediate aftermath of my departure, La Russa chose to accept it. He understood that this thing had ridden me long enough, that my really bad day had become countless worse ones. It was time for me to go, and for the organization to let go.

All things considered, I thought I was pretty well adjusted. I mean, I was screwed up and everything, I couldn't throw a ball sixty feet without practically breaking out in hives, and I'd become expert in medicating my ghosts so at least I could survive the harrowing hours around the ball games. But, hey, fake it till you make it. To the end, I'd shown up every day, and worked to get it right and held on to the hope I'd make it, and now I was in my midtwenties and could think of no reason at the moment to get off the couch.

Harvey believed I was, his words here, *that psychological tire*. I'd been riding hard miles on that tire for four and a half years, and the tire was worn and road-weary and quite possibly dangerous. He also believed I would know when the journey, that being my career, was done. He'd never said, "Ank, it ain't gonna happen," even if he'd known it. And he did know it. He got me through the day, however, and then went to work on the next day, and he prepared me for what he knew was the inevitable.

Harvey would tell Scott the time was coming when the tire would blow. They had to be ready with an alternative to the lives I'd once had—the one I'd been chasing for four and a half years and the one I'd escaped before that. I thought Harvey was being my shrink, being my friend, being my father figure. He thought he was saving my life.

The phone rang. It was Scott. *Geez*, I thought, *I'm fine.* I picked up.

"How's it going?" he asked.

This again.

"I'm good, Scott," I said.

"You sure?"

"I'm fine."

"Ank," he said, "you ready to go play?"

"Go play what? I'm done." Wasn't he listening? Wasn't anybody?

"Outfield. For the Cardinals. I talked to Walt."

Wait. What?

"Jocketty," I said. "You talked to Walt Jocketty, and he wants me to play the outfield. For the Cardinals."

"Yes."

"You're not bullshitting me, are you?"

"You're a big leaguer," Scott said. "You can do this. They'll start you on the minor-league side. You'll work your way up. It'll work. You're good enough."

Scott and Harvey had worked this out. Harvey had advised against it, against inviting more failure, unless Scott was absolutely sure I could return to the major leagues. A five-year minor-league slog, topping out in Double A, sending me back to the couch again at thirty years old, would only put more miles on that same psychological tire.

"When have I ever been anything but up-front with you?" Scott chided.

"I know. I know I know I know."

"You can do this. Go have a good time. Go beat the game. You'd be great."

Damn, I'd just quit baseball. Three hours before, I'd said good-bye. No regrets. I sat up, looked around, found the poster. *Who do I trust?*

I hit in high school. I hit a little in the big leagues, when pitchers figured there'd be nothing to lose by throwing me fastballs. I did hit some in the minors. That was rookie ball. Against kids. I wasn't an everyday player. I hadn't played the outfield since Port St. Lucie. This was crazy. Beyond crazy. But I was twenty-five. Wasn't that when regular people started their careers? It would never work. But it might.

I tried to clear my head. Was I ready to fall back in love with baseball? Was I going to do this to myself again? Didn't I want to sleep?

"They wanted me?"

"This isn't charity," Scott said. "You can play. You can do this."

"OK, lemme think."

"Ank, I believe in this. I think you should too."

"When?"

"Tomorrow."

Well, damn.

"Tomorrow, huh?"

For the first time that day, I let a little of the outside world in. I went to my computer.

Lory Bailey grew up in Deerfield Beach, on the coast about halfway between Miami and Fort Pierce. She lived a little north of there, in Delray Beach, about a half hour south of Jupiter. A mutual friend introduced us. I found her beautiful and strong-willed and smart and refreshingly unimpressed with what I did for a living, because at that particular time I wasn't so sure myself. She'd never heard of me before we met. Of course, there was no reason she should have. Still, to her, I wasn't *that guy*, which I was to plenty of other people.

Lory had been a Miami Dolphins cheerleader, loved sports, and understood that a certain amount of selfishness is required to play the game well, but that didn't mean she was going to live with it. We'd met a month before. She didn't mind my house having a Ping-Pong table where the dining room table should have been. In fact, she thought it was great, and I thought she was great for thinking it was great. Maybe she believed the video game/jukebox thingy in the living room was a little over the top, and the red carpet was a bit too much like, well, red carpet, but she didn't let on, and we listened to the same music— country, hip-hop, whatever. We watched *Forrest Gump* until we could recite the lines to each other before Forrest did. One day, Lory would walk down the aisle to the theme song—"Feather"—from the movie. Sometimes she even sat through *Scarface*.

Lory was game for a sports bar, which I confirmed on one of our first dates, or for an afternoon on a wave-thrown boat on the ocean. On the back of the boat, I handed her a rod with a fish on the end of it, and she reeled in a three-foot spinner shark like she'd been born for it. "I grew up on a canal," she said, answering my surprise. "There were fish in my backyard." I didn't have to hide from her the rising anxiety of the coming baseball season because it dissolved when I was with her. It was simple like that. We were simple like that.

I had my father to bear. She had lost hers when she was eight years old, to a drunk driver so many New Year's Eves before.

So I sent her cards that she'd keep forever. And when we weren't together, we'd be talking on the phone or instant messaging on the computer. We were a month into this thing, and it was perfect, and we both thought so, so I figured I should tell her I'd quit my job, and then Scott had called and I'd sort of, maybe, possibly unquit. I signed on to the computer, and there she was.

We typed back and forth about nothing, really, just life, and Lory gave me an opening.

"Can't take anything for granted," she wrote about something.

"Speaking of that," I lunged.

"Yessss . . . "

"I've been thinking about this for a couple weeks. Just trying to make sure what the right thing would be to do. For me to be truly happy. And I came to my decision today. And I retired from pitching. Gonna announce it to the media tomorrow. I'm gonna trust you to keep that between me and you. But it's just not fun for me anymore."

"Wow," she typed.

"I know."

"If you are sure that is what you want to do, I'm with ya sweetheart. You have to do what ultimately makes you happy."

"That's exactly what I came to."

"Well I'm happy for you then. I'm sure it was a hard decision. Do you know what direction you want to go in, or did you just know that wasn't what you wanted to do?"

"I feel better already."

"Good," she wrote. "I'm happy if you are happy."

"Knew it wasn't what I wanted to do. . . . I might move to a position."

There was a pause before Lory answered.

"Can you hit?"

I laughed. "Don't try me like that."

I told her I'd see her tomorrow, signed off, and smiled. *I can hit*, I thought. *Right? I mean, I can probably hit.* I stood and walked to the window, sensed the snook again, knew they were out there fighting. I thought about the game, what it had once been to me, and I felt it again in my heart. Not racing this time but swelling. I was going to be a ballplayer again. A real ballplayer.

Can I hit?

Hell, yes.

CHAPTER
TWENTY-ONE

I slept that night, all the way through, and woke up dazed. After a minute or two, first spent wondering why I was so rested, it occurred to me that I was an outfielder today, as of right then, and that I didn't have to pitch today, or tomorrow, or ever again, and it was so crazy and wonderful it might work. If I'd dreamed, I could not remember of what. I paused at a window, looked down into the backyard, and thought, *I should have that wall fixed*. I looked around at a world that would never have me throw another pitch, the choice I'd made twenty-four hours before, and was offering more. A do-over. All I'd had to do to get there was donate eight years of my life, some self-esteem, several prime years of baseball, a biological father, an elbow, countless deep breaths, and parts of a cinder-block wall.

I was good with that. I'd tried. I'd not regret a moment of the effort to be the next Koufax, even when it was hopeless, even if I could've started taking fly balls and batting practice all those years ago. If this was the journey, then point out the path. Pitching the way I had, living with it as I had, had brought me to here, and taught me to forget yesterday, and reminded me there could be no shame in effort. Nobody had worked harder over those eight years, of that I was sure, and no reasonably healthy person had endured more. Yeah, I was a wreck for a long time. And, yeah, I showed up every stinkin' day to wear it, or beat it, or survive it.

That made me the guy who would do the improbable, and already in my head I could hear those who would not believe.

A pitcher. Is going to be an outfielder. A pitcher. Is going to try to hit. At twenty-five years old. Good luck with that. Wait'll the sliders come—they'll make the Thing look like a puppy dog.

That only made it more fun. The pressure was gone. You boys want to bring the cameras? The notepads? The questions? Bring 'em on over here. Psshht, hell, yeah, I can hit. I think. I mean, let's go find out.

The drive the morning before, when I'd handed in my uniform, was all but forgotten. They'd just give it back. I had my bats, had a general idea where center field was, had Lory beside me, had Harvey behind me, and had a whole career before me. My mind was so clear I could've sworn my head was lighter, and I sang along to the radio like a man who could actually sing. I waved to the security guard, now thoroughly perplexed.

Babe Ruth, of course, I knew about, he having been a pitcher for five notable years and a twenty-game winner for a couple of them and otherwise about the best hitter ever. As a Cardinal, I'd heard Stan Musial had started as a pitcher before becoming an outfielder, a Hall of Famer, and a legend in St. Louis. Other than that, the examples of men who'd walked off the mound and into the batter's box with any sort of success were rare. There were first basemen and outfielders and catchers who pitched in high school and college. There were plenty who went the other way, catchers and outfielders who found breaking balls were easier to throw than hit. And there were more— those who ascended to the mound or descended from it— who failed.

"First day, Harv," I said on the phone on the way over.

"Go get 'em, kid," he said.

"I will."

Standing in the clubhouse that morning, some guys had heard about my change in plans, others said, "Yer gonna what?" and a few hadn't realized I'd been gone the day before.

"So, yeah," I told them, "I've had kind of a weird twenty-four hours," before bursting into laughter.

I couldn't recall being in higher spirits. Man, it was good to be out from under that burden and in that locker room, with those guys, a whole day waiting. I wasn't afraid. If there were any nerves, they registered low on my personal anxiety scale, right there with what I was going to have for lunch and whether the orange crop was going to come in OK this year.

On the sheets of paper tacked to the corkboard, "Ankiel" was not listed under bullpens or sprints or pitchers' fielding practice—or my personal domain, which was unspoken and unwritten: Hey, Ank, get here at dawn so nobody can watch.

Today it was "Hey, Ank, go hit with the A-ball guys, then go hit with the Double-A guys, then see you in the cages, just keep piling up at bats."

I went to Jim Edmonds.

"Whatta you think?" I said.

"Well," he said, "you're gonna need this."

He handed me an outfielder's glove, bigger than the one I used for pitching.

"And use this," he said.

He gave me a tiny glove, not even a foot long, that he used as a training tool. Catch enough fungoes and batting-practice fly balls in that, the regular glove will feel like a butterfly net.

"Anything else?"

"Good luck, Ank. Good to have you on our side."

"Thanks, man."

I gathered up a couple bats, a pair of metal spikes, and my two new gloves and ran off to my new career, wearing a smile you could have seen from St. Louis, or Johnson City, or Knoxville, or my own backyard.

CHAPTER
TWENTY-TWO

I arrived early. I stayed late. I soaked my aching body. I bandaged my bubbled and bloody hands. I shagged fly balls so earnestly that the other outfielders began bunching in left and right fields, leaving me to chase the demons away.

The second day, with the A ballers, I had four hits in six at bats, and it was fun. Even when I'd pitched better at the end, when I'd ground it hard enough to get back to the big leagues and walk off a mound with some satisfaction, it hadn't ever been fun anymore. That, maybe, was the part of me I'd missed the most, even more than the great, effortless pitcher I'd felt I could be. I'd missed being able to enjoy it. I'd missed looking forward to the next game. I'd missed racing into the outfield gap, not sure you could reach a ball but maybe you could, and I'd missed the hours it would take to get a swing just how you liked it, then backspinning a ball so pure you hadn't even felt the contact. Mostly, I'd missed competing against the other guy rather than competing against myself, getting back to a game that would be settled by the width of the ball and the breadth of the man.

I knew I'd make it. Absolutely knew it. But if by some force of humankind or nature I didn't, hell, it would be satisfaction enough to have had a good time trying. So I stood across from Dave McKay, an exceptional outfield coach, and put my feet where he told me to, and began to learn to become a big-league center fielder. And I hit off a tee, and hit soft-toss, and hit BP fastballs, and faced real pitchers, and began to learn to be a big-league hitter.

When I saw a smirk, or even imagined one, or read a sentence about what a long shot this was, or listened to the radio long enough to learn what a valiant yet futile effort I'd undertaken, I'd show up ten minutes earlier the next day and make up ten minutes on whoever thought their job was safe.

All I had to do was avoid the sixty-foot throws, which wasn't so hard. It was going to be OK to fail once in a while anyway, which was liberating.

The Cardinals started me in Double A as the everyday right fielder in Springfield, Missouri. I struck out a lot. So they restarted me in Single A as the everyday right fielder and occasional center fielder for Quad Cities in Davenport, Iowa. After two months, they sent me back to Springfield. When the season ended, I was a .259 hitter with a .339 on-base percentage and, in 369 at bats, 21 home runs. I wasn't

Babe Ruth, but neither was I a pitcher trying to survive a game that was over my head, and neither was it a gimmick. The outfield grass felt good under my feet, and throwing a ball two hundred feet or three hundred feet was a lot easier than throwing it sixty feet, six inches, and I'd live with the cruelty that it could be a lot more accurate too.

The winter brought opportunity. I could prepare like an outfielder. I could lift weights like a hitter. If I could produce in Double A, and I was by the end, then Triple A was only a matter of getting stronger and smarter, and piling at bats on at bats, and reading the line drive that was going to top-spin dive in front of me or backspin over my head. There was catching up to do, which meant settling into a single set of hitting mechanics and swinging until they became second nature, and then separating the sliders from the fastballs and the cutters from the rest, and that was going to be the hard part. I'd always thought great hitters are born and yet don't become truly great until they're holding a wood bat under dim lights in a little town where the mosquitoes are big enough to carry away a hot dog, chili and all. That's where the habits are formed, the ones that settle your heart when the pitcher has won two hundred big-league games and has seen plenty like you and isn't the least impressed. I remembered feeling that way about lots of hitters, and I won only thirteen games—one of them with the help of a bucket of vodka.

My objective, then, was to cram seven years, those formative years for hitters, into one off-season, and I walked into spring training in 2006 with the other position players feeling like I was physically ready to compete. What

I'd need was gamelike at bats, and there'd be plenty of those over the course of spring training, so I stood amid Jim Edmonds, Juan Encarnación, So Taguchi, and Skip Schumaker, feeling like my bat would play and knowing my glove and arm would. Whatever Jimmy did, I did. Where he went, I followed. What Darryl Kile had been to me as a pitcher, Jimmy had become to me as an outfielder, the kind of selflessness I never forgot. I was still working on footwork in the outfield and staying short to the ball in the batter's box, but it was coming, and I could still hit a ball a long way. I hadn't left that in high school.

The 2005 Cardinals had won one hundred games and lost in the National League Championship Series to the Houston Astros. The sense in St. Louis was that the 2006 team could be at least as good. I wanted to be a part of that, and that drove me through the early part of camp until, one morning two days before our exhibition opener, Tony La Russa stopped me and said, "You're starting in center in the first game." I was going to be in a big-league game—in March, in a spring-training ballpark, but still— as the center fielder for the Cardinals, a huge honor, and if not for the nagging ache in my knee, everything would have been perfect.

Turned out, the patellar tendon was torn. They sent me for surgery, then months of rehabilitation, and by the time I was sturdy over that knee again, I was preparing for 2007. They were right about the '06 Cardinals, by the way. While I was bringing my knee back to life, they were winning the World Series. Albert Pujols was great. Chris Carpenter was great. I got another scar.

CHAPTER
TWENTY-THREE

My father was released from prison around then. He'd been led away when I was a twenty-year-old pitcher. He returned when I was a twenty-seven-year-old outfielder, my pitching career long gone, all of which had happened without him.

He called one night, having wrangled my number from somewhere, and attempted what sounded maybe like an apology, something along the theme of it being all his fault because he'd gone to jail and it would have been different if he'd been there for me. And I was tired of him already.

I hung up, hoping that was the end of it, sure it wouldn't be. I worried for my mother. She stayed closer to the house than she would with my father locked up, fearing now a chance meeting. The past six years had been good for her, and now she had to think about where she was going, whom she might run into. It was starting again.

Lory and I would be married that winter, on New Year's Eve. The nearer the wedding drew, the more she missed her father. Being a kind soul, she gently suggested that I invite my father back into my life. The years, maybe, had changed him. Or maybe not. But wasn't it worth finding out? You get one father. Our children, when we had them, would get only one grandfather. There'd be no harm trying to forgive him, and perhaps the prospect of rebuilding a relationship with me, meeting Lory, would lead him to treat my mother with decency.

"You're in a different place now, Ank," Harvey said. "I can't see the harm."

So I called my father, invited him to my bachelor party, and saved him a seat on a bus that would ferry about a dozen of us to bars around town. This was to be a celebratory ride with some of the closest friends I had, a night for us to bond and laugh and forget about the real world for a while.

It wasn't.

I was a grown man, different from the boy my father had abused with words and deeds, more courageous than the boy who'd seen his mother terrorized. I'd lived enough of my adulthood to understand I wasn't always in charge, that all I could do was work hard, throw hard, and hope for the best. "It's not your fault," Harvey would say, and that's different from "It's not your destiny" or "There's not a damned thing you can do about it" or "Eh, who cares?"

I cared. And I was in charge now. And he was here because I allowed it. He sat across the bus aisle, surrounded by men in their prime, young and strong. My father was an old man, and I sensed he knew it. Not in the years, maybe, but in the miles. He moved with an effort I didn't recall. His laugh came from a place farther away, and the conversation left him behind, the context lost over a six-year prison term. His attempts at familiarity were forced and clumsy.

Within a few blocks, I knew I'd made a mistake. After a few beers, the mistake only got louder, and the man I remembered was sitting across from me. I, however, was not the son he remembered. It's possible we came to that understanding in the same moment, that he would live forever in my eyes as the father who was cruel and selfish and, ultimately, forgotten. He hadn't earned me as a son any more than he'd earned that night in the bus, toasting a woman I would love and marry and treat with dignity. There's stuff you don't get to say I'm sorry for.

"I'm sorry," he said anyway, and I went cold.

The bus sighed to a stop at the curb. The music thumped from behind large windows, on the other side of which was a bar crowded with people laughing and carrying on. Yes, a night for celebration, and the whole town would celebrate with us, and my friends piled from the bus and across the sidewalk and into that place.

"Son," he said.

"What?"

"We need to talk."

"Now. You want to talk now. Tonight." Not a question.

"I need to explain."

So it was him, me, and up ahead somewhere a bus driver pretending not to listen.

His mouth moved, and I didn't hear. I thought about his taking this night, my night, and making it his. Just like he'd taken my childhood. Like he'd made my baseball his baseball. My success had to be his success. My failures were somebody else's.

His mouth moved, and I thought, *This is all so dumb.* Nothing had changed, except I wasn't afraid and he wasn't so sure of himself anymore. Nobody was screaming for her life. The cops were off chasing somebody else. My friends were inside having a grand time while I dealt with my father, and even years later, they'd remember the night on the bus and say, "We had a good time. We know you didn't, but the rest of us did," and they'd laugh at the absurdity of the guy who said he was sorry twenty years too late. At my bachelor party. I wasn't mad. I was just over it.

I'd invited him out of obligation. I sat in a dark bus out of obligation. Those years were hard on him too, he said, and I listened out of obligation, for what I didn't know. Maybe I was still hoping I was wrong about him, the evidence notwithstanding. Maybe I was hoping to protect my mother, best I could, that he'd behave if a relationship with his son were in the balance.

I was wrong.

I don't miss him. I miss the notion of a father, though. The notion of a grandfather for my children, the man who'd put $20 in an envelope and scratch out, "Don't spend it all in one place," like an inside joke, out of kindness. I would've loved that.

CHAPTER
TWENTY-FOUR

The road back to the big leagues, turned out, concluded with 270 miles due north on Interstate 55 in a maroon Ford F-150 pickup truck, Lory behind the wheel, me dozing beside her, a bat bag in the back.

We didn't stop between Memphis and St. Louis. We hardly slowed down.

I walked into the clubhouse, and the men there stood and applauded. Most of them I knew. Some I didn't. They clapped me on the back. I laughed and shook their hands and asked where they kept the bats.

I'd last been a major leaguer on October 1, 2004. I'd been a major leaguer for thirty-four innings, not even four full games' worth, since the 2000 season, since the Thing came and got me.

When Lory wished me luck and let me out at Busch Stadium, it was the middle of the afternoon, August 9, 2007.

I was twenty-eight years old. A good part of my prime had been spent chasing the pitcher inside me. Unless, you know, it had been chasing me all along. It was complicated. The rest, the past couple years, was this. That is, chasing the hitter inside me. Chasing the big leagues again. Swinging hard. Hitting 32 home runs in 102 games at Triple-A Memphis. Kicking the crap out of the monster.

The night before, I'd been in Tacoma with the Memphis Redbirds. The flight back to Tennessee had been canceled. We wouldn't leave until midnight. So we went to dinner, then we sat at the airport and waited. My teammates and I filled the time the way young, bored men generally fill the time: we drank beer. We were delayed a while.

Somewhere in and among the beers, Chris Maloney—"Hammer" to us—tapped me on the shoulder. Hammer was our manager and a very good man.

"Bull," he said, which is what he called me, because Hammer was country like that, "you're going to the Show."

I looked Hammer in the eye, because I needed to be sure he hadn't gotten this wrong, and I needed to be absolutely clear on what he'd said, and I replied, "What?"

"Yeah, Bull," he said. "They want you there tomorrow night. You're starting in right."

Well, damn. I'd have another beer to that.

I called Lory. She said she was proud of me and that she'd be waiting for me at home.

I called Harvey. He said I'd be great. I called Scott. I called a man named Bob Brower, a former big-league outfielder who worked for Scott and had been a mentor when I needed one, then a friend when I needed one of those more.

I called my mother. She asked what time she should be in St. Louis.

We boarded at last, a single plane flight remaining in a comeback that had started on a couch in Jupiter, Florida, and across two and a half years overlaid in countless batting cages and batter's boxes. This was the flight I thought about when the sliders were unhittable and the line drives were caught and my hands were so sore they begged for a day off. This was the flight Rick Eckstein and I talked about when we were done hitting, sometimes for two hours after games. He was a hitting coach, only much more than that. He was as obsessed as I was and worked as hard as I did. That meant off days. That meant we turned the lights out nearly every night. That meant long talks on what pitchers would see in me, and what they'd go after, and just how I was going to make up all the time I'd missed in the batter's box. This flight didn't happen without Rick Eckstein. The notion of this flight—out there somewhere—had replaced the nightmares. And so when it was time, I hauled a bag down the aisle, reached the appointed row, and between the two largest, hairiest people I'd ever seen discovered the sliver of a middle seat that would carry me back to the big leagues.

Hell, I would've flown on the wing.

I got skinny, squeezed in, put my head back, closed my eyes. When I opened them again, I'd be that much closer to right field at Busch Stadium.

"Ank."

Chris Conway was our trainer.

I opened my eyes. We weren't in Memphis. I could tell because my seat space was still full of oversized strangers.

"Ank, take my seat," he said. "Got a big day tomorrow. You'll need some rest."

"Really? Where?"

"Exit-row window."

"Dude . . . "

There are some kind people in this world.

We flew through the night. When I reached Memphis, Lory had moved our stuff from the apartment to the truck. All of it. She was ready to go. I was nervous, but I smiled a lot. Scott Boras was right. Harvey Dorfman was right. I was right. I'd survived the cutters. I'd resurrected my game on the other side of the ball, discovered my arm was a lot more accurate from three hundred feet than it was from sixty, and learned to love being a ballplayer again.

I'd left a pitcher, returned an outfielder, and I was just, for the moment, so proud of myself. They'd wanted a tough kid, a product of his environment instead of a victim of it, a survivor, a young man who refused to walk away, who'd fight for his place in the world, and what they got was a right fielder who'd bat second—between David Eckstein, Rick's younger brother, and Albert Pujols— against the San Diego Padres that night.

I wanted to be great. The goal from the start was not merely to make my way back to the big leagues but to go be somebody in the big leagues. Still, I couldn't be great from Memphis. I couldn't be great if nobody else believed. I couldn't be great just because I tried hard and almost made it.

I'd called ahead to let the Cardinals know I'd be there and asked Rip Rowan, the clubhouse manager, if number 24 were available. Nope, I was told. Joe Pettini, Tony La Russa's bench coach, had 24.

"Give me whatever, then," I'd said. "Doesn't matter. Just be sure it's on a major-league uniform."

I pulled open the door to a major-league clubhouse I'd sometimes wondered if I'd ever see again. The man on the lineup card was me. The uniform in the locker—white, red, and beautiful—had my name on the back. Along with the number 24. *Good guy, Joe*, I thought. *I missed this*, I thought: the camaraderie, the people who looked out for you. The selfless ones.

In the bottom of the first inning, I stood in the on-deck circle, twirling my bat, listening to the crowd call my name, trying not to relive the journey and failing. That mound and me. That backstop and me. That game. That pitch. And look at me now. I was here for a million reasons. I'd worked for it. I'd believed when there were no other options. Harvey had believed. Scott too. And Lory, who'd come along at just the right time.

The rush from Tacoma to Memphis to right field in St. Louis was due, in part, to the sudden absence of Scott Spiezio, a veteran outfielder who'd left to seek treatment for substance abuse. The number on my right arm, a white 32 in a circle of black, was for Josh Hancock, who'd died in an April car crash. I'd been on one of those minor-league

buses when somebody in the back had said, "Hey, somebody on the Cardinals died," and held up his phone, and
what I thought of was Darryl Kile, his wife and his children, and how not being able to throw strikes amounts to
nothing.

David Eckstein walked. It was my turn. With a deep
breath, I walked toward the plate. A standing ovation rose
around me. They'd ridden along for a good portion of
this crossing. I'd have bet plenty of them had been here
on that afternoon in October, a lifetime ago, too. I wasn't
sure how this was going to go, but I was glad they were
here with me. It felt like home. Lory was up there too, and
I could feel her eyes on me.

In front of almost forty-three thousand people, I stood
in against Padres right-hander Chris Young and popped
to shortstop. Two innings later, I struck out. In the fifth
inning, I struck out again. In the seventh inning, the Cardinals led, 2–0. We'd scored earlier in the inning on, of all
things, a wild pitch. Two runners were on base, two out,
the veteran reliever Doug Brocail pitching. The count was
two balls, one strike.

For some moments over the previous twenty hours, it
would have been enough to be here, to pull a long breath
of it. But not in that moment.

Brocail threw a slider. Down in the strike zone. Outside. I button-hooked it. We called that kind of swing
"walking the dog," a low, easy yank of the wrists. Just
leaned over the plate, got the bat barrel on it, hit it hard,
felt the contact, heard the contact, lost my top hand a little, pulled it to right field, and what I thought was *I got*

your ass. Nothing personal, but *Holy shit, I got your ass.* A three-run home run. The following day, a Dodgers player—the Dodgers already were in town for the next series—said he'd heard a roar from his downtown hotel room and wondered what had transpired.

Almost seven years after it had happened the first time, I felt as though I'd left my body again. This time, however, there was no panic. My breaths were short. Not out of fear but in celebration. In joy. I could feel the game in my heart, in my soul. This time, I ran the bases on somebody else's legs, watching from above. This time, I was cheering like the rest.

When it was done and I was in the dugout with my teammates again and the people out there wouldn't stop chanting my name, and when I rose to the top step to say thank you to those who were kind enough to remember me, I felt no pain. What I felt was strength. Power. Energy. The game was good again. And I was good at it again.

My heart was smiling. And I wanted everyone to see.

The game wasn't over, and yet Tony La Russa stood by the dugout steps, applauding and smiling. I didn't recall ever seeing that before. Nobody could.

"Holy smokes," Tony said to himself. "Holy smokes."

Years later, he would recall it as "one of the happiest days of my life." He went on, "I would tell my grandson or granddaughter, I'd say, 'How much of a story do you want to know? Do you just want to know the baseball-player part of it, as exciting a pitching-potential superstar as your granddad has seen, sixty years of baseball, who, in your granddad's opinion, got dealt a very unfair set of circumstances that curtailed that great potential? This guy had gifts of strength of character, determination that matched his physical gifts, and came back as an outfielder. He got back to the big leagues, and that's a pretty damned good success. Yes, a very tough set of circumstances growing up, but not making excuses, not being a bum on the street, and here he is a father of two, so I love him. I just will never quit hoping that he had a good quality of life.'"

I stood before reporters afterward and went along with the story, because it was the only one I had. I kept it short. Lory was waiting. And I was tired, not just twenty-four-hour tired but seven-year tired, like I could sleep for a month.

"I was young, and I don't think I understood the magnitude of what was going on," I told them. "That seems like a long time ago. It's ancient. I'm a different guy. I was so young then."

I looked around, past the cameras.

"I guess we all were."

We laughed.

I met Lory at the hotel and fell back on the bed. She handed me a glass of wine. We answered text messages from friends and marveled at the long, strange trip. While living those seven years, they'd seemed so slow, like such a grind, that nothing had ever been easy. From that hotel room, however, they'd passed in a snap of our fingers, like just yesterday I'd stood in that very ballpark sorting the real threats from the imagined ones. I had changed, I decided. I was a better version of myself. Lory was part of that. Harvey wouldn't have had it any other way. I hoped he'd seen that home run. I was sure he had.

"Want me to turn this on?" Lory asked, holding the television remote.

She knew my aversion to sports-highlight shows. They'd had a little too much fun at my expense over the years.

"Why not?" I said.

They called me "the Natural." We watched the same scene over and over, from this angle or that one, and I was struck by how happy I looked. More, how happy the people in the stands looked. Tony La Russa, mouth hanging open, as though he could hardly believe it. Jimmy Edmonds on the top step, the first to greet me at the dugout. Sitting finally on the bench not far from Adam Kennedy, who had signed back with the Cardinals, his smile nearly matching mine.

Two days later, I homered twice against the Dodgers in front of a huge crowd, including two guys I knew from middle school—Charlie Pratt and Jerry Seidel—who'd flown in. By the end of August, I was hitting .328 with five home runs. I went to Houston, site of my misguided effort to circumvent the monster, and had three hits in a game, six in a three-game series.

Every day was better than the last.

CHAPTER
TWENTY-FIVE

I was in the Mitchell Report, from the middle of page 243 to the top of page 244. The three paragraphs that reported my name and my use of human growth hormone (HGH) from January 2004 to December of that year are accurate. I bought HGH and injected it.

All true.

The Mitchell Report was the result of a nearly two-year investigation by George Mitchell, the former US senator. It was funded by Major League Baseball (MLB) and released in December 2007. About ninety players were named. I was near the top, you know, alphabetically. The stars were Roger Clemens, Barry Bonds, José Canseco, Jason Giambi, and the shadowy men who supplied drugs to dozens of big leaguers.

The report was released on a rainy day in Manhattan, where Mitchell himself stood before reporters in a crowded Midtown hotel conference room and explained his findings. The commissioner, Bud Selig, sat nearby. This was big news. I didn't pay it much mind.

Four years before, I'd undergone Tommy John surgery, the elbow procedure that puts pitchers' careers back in order. Recovery requires about a year. During that period, a guy I knew at my gym suggested HGH, which he believed would promote healing. He gave me the address of a doctor in Palm Beach. I went home and looked up HGH. I read through MLB's list of banned substances. No HGH. I read on the Internet about the benefits of HGH. It sounded new age. It would help my elbow heal faster and stronger. I wondered if it would heal my mind too.

Within a few days, I was at the doctor's office, submitting to a variety of exams, including a blood test, that the doctor and I both knew would lead to a prescription for HGH. If I could take something that would put me on a mound sooner, that would make me of some use to the Cardinals a few weeks early, that was not prohibited by the league, then, yeah, sign me up.

My first dose arrived. I paid with a check. Several tubes came in a box. A powder and gel were in each tube, separated by a seal. The idea was to twist the tube, break the seal, allow the powder and the gel to mix and then push the needle into my skin, which weirded me out some but wasn't so bad after a while.

I did this for almost a year. I did not return faster than the rehabilitation schedule in the pages of that binder said

I would. I did get leaner, so there was that. I looked better in a bathing suit.

I took HGH because it was, by MLB standards, legal. I told no one. In 2005, when MLB banned HGH, I stopped using HGH.

A couple years later, in September 2007, the clinic where I received my HGH got busted, because the pharmacy from where it got its HGH got busted, because the Albany, New York, district attorney's office had investigated and busted a ring of dealers who sold performance-enhancing drugs on the Internet. And I had paid with a check, which is how I ended up with my day at the center of a decadelong performance-enhancing-drugs conversation. I was not part of the investigation, other than being identified as a customer (along with about a dozen other ballplayers), and I was in no legal jeopardy. I didn't see what the issue was.

So, on what otherwise was one of the best nights of my baseball life—I'd hit 2 home runs and had 7 RBI in Pittsburgh and was as of then batting .358 with 9 homers and 29 RBI across 24 games—a clubhouse attendant sidled up to me in the dugout and said, "Walt Jocketty's on the phone in the video room. Wants to talk to you," and the Cardinals general manager told me there'd be a story in the next day's *New York Daily News* reporting that I had used HGH all those years ago.

This, just in time for my return to the major leagues as a hitter, just in time for me enjoying—really enjoying— baseball again, just in time for all the other stories calling me the Natural, and just in time to slip me onto pages 243 and 244 of the Mitchell Report.

So that sucked. First, because I felt I'd done nothing illegal. Second, because it was forever ago, before anyone—myself included—knew much about HGH. And third, because I'd managed to go, like, a whole month thinking only about baseball, and now I was in a dugout in Phoenix having reporters ask me leading questions about cheating, and a couple days later I'd be in a hotel conference room being interrogated by MLB investigators and FBI agents. The fact that I was not in trouble legally or, ultimately, with the league seemed lost on everyone.

Did it bother me? I didn't think so. But I also hit .069 for the next week and a half.

CHAPTER
TWENTY-SIX

Among the many wonders of the monster was its attention to the elements of time, space, and various other dimensions, leaving, for example, the following absurdity:

Throw the ball from sixty feet, and it will come out fluttering and crazy, like a pigeon with one wing. If you shot the pigeon 95 mph out of a cannon.

But if I threw the ball from 250 feet, it would be beautiful. Pure. True. A bullet's trajectory. A laser's precision. An artist's flair.

This makes little sense, but then, none of it did.

Maybe it was the freedom to simply let it fly. Maybe it was the lack of expectation. Two hundred and fifty feet—or more—is a long way to throw a baseball with any reasonable hope for perfection. From the center-field wall to third base, you don't think *glove* any more than you'd stand 180 yards out on a fairway and think *hole*. You think *rhythm*. You think *vicinity*. Sometimes you think *cutoff man*, but that's not nearly as fun.

Distance—really, anything at one hundred feet or more—was my friend. While maybe I could have continued to survive at sixty, tiptoeing through every day like I'd been, from one hundred feet, two hundred feet, more, the ball felt right in my hand again. The game looked right in my head. That arm Tony La Russa had once fawned over, it was still there, still attached, still strong and capable. The love-hate period with that arm was over the moment I picked up a bigger glove, set up deep on the outfield grass, and started hunting fly balls and base runners.

Inside, I begged them to run.

On the days I got a couple hits and on the days I didn't, I could still run after a baseball. I could still hold a wary man at first base. I could still go get the reckless man at third. That was the game like it used to be. Just the game. No more obsessing over it. No more counting breaths. I was still surviving in some ways, the usual ways that come with an unusual life, but I was competing in most. And when I returned to the big leagues, when my understanding for what it had required of me had matched my gratitude for it, there'd be nights when the game was so familiar again. Swing the bat, run the bases, catch the ball, throw it, and count 'em up at the end.

Just baseball, you know? Man, I'd missed it.

So it was on May 6, 2008, Coors Field in Colorado, the Cardinals having won twenty-one of their first thirty-three games, me in center field. The lousy part about me in center field was that I'd replaced my friend Jim Edmonds, who'd been important in my transition from pitcher to outfielder. One of the great athletes and center fielders in the league while in his prime, a World Series champion and a four-time All-Star, he also was coming up on thirty-eight years old. He'd taught me things I couldn't learn anywhere else, how to feel the game. We'd talked for hours about instincts and hunches and what those meant for standing in exactly the right area at exactly the right time when the baseball came down.

Then he was traded to the San Diego Padres for David Freese, a young third baseman who one day would find his own place in Cardinals lore.

The great part about me being in center field was, well, I was in center field. For the Cardinals. I was playing every day, hitting with some success, and, on this particular night, making two throws from the outfield that would help win a ball game. My arm was winning games again, and that, even amid an inch-at-a-time baseball season that leaves almost no time for self-assessment, felt like something worth honoring.

First inning, runners at first and second, Rockies burner Willy Taveras the lead runner, one out. Fly ball to deep center field. Second baseman Adam Kennedy standing on his base, arms over his head. The idea here, in almost all circumstances, is to keep the trailing runner from moving up to second. Almost nobody throws to third. It's not the play. But, man, he was gonna run on me? On me?

So I threw out Taveras. A tracer shot, my hand to Troy Glaus's glove. On the fly. If Glaus hadn't caught the ball, it would've hit the bag. Inning over. Threat over. The place went crazy.

When I reached the dugout, teammates were shaking their heads and laughing. I loved it.

Tony La Russa, who held a somewhat unnatural love for the cutoff man, came over, smiled, and said, "That was awesome. Don't ever do it again."

Maybe he was joking. Probably not.

It was a once-in-a-season throw. Maybe once in a career. It was my second-best throw of the night.

Omar Quintanilla hit a line drive to left-center field. The ball landed in the grass, skipped, bounced a few times, and rolled to the wall. Coors Field's outfield is massive by design, due to the lack of gravity or something. A ball to left-center field is a triple almost every time. By the time I'd gathered the ball and registered our left fielder, Ryan Ludwick, shouting, "Three! Three! Three!" I was so far from third base I could barely see it. But I knew it was there.

A crow hop, and I let it fly. As far and hard as I could throw a ball. Why not? Why not try? I thought, *That's the one.* Just *That's the one.* I knew it was going to be good. Really good. The ball cleared two cutoff men, the crowd began to groan as it realized that ball and its base runner were now in a dead heat, and then the ball arrived at Glaus head high just as Quintanilla arrived on his belly. He was out too, a thunderbolt from left-center.

And the conversation began about my arm again, and whether it was the best outfield arm in the league, and I couldn't help but smile at such a thing. This was the same arm that had almost run me from the league. The same arm that had inspired so many career obituaries.

The thing was, I never thought about mechanics anymore, because I trusted them. I didn't worry about where the ball would go, because I trusted it. I did occasionally worry about what La Russa thought, but put me in the moment, give me the ball and a daring base runner and a crowd wishing for something magical, and I would attempt that throw. "Let it eat," we'd say. "You gotta let it eat."

A couple years later, Braves manager Bobby Cox was quoted as saying, "He has the best outfield arm I have ever seen—better than Rocky Colavito, Ellis Valentine, Bill Robinson, you name 'em."

He loved Colavito, but Cox said, "I've never seen anybody throw like [Ankiel]."

That was enough for me. It made my day, that someone would say something like that. That it was Bobby Cox, one of my boyhood heroes? Days don't come better. Damn, that arm had almost sucked the soul straight out of me. But I wouldn't let it. And a few years later, it was a good part of the reason I was back and aimed to stay.

CHAPTER
TWENTY-SEVEN

Late on a Friday night one October, tucked in against the San Francisco Bay, I resisted counting the steps along the way. There were too many. The stories were too long and too complicated, even composed and recomposed in my own head.

A decade and six days had passed since I'd stood on that mound in St. Louis and come undone. And yet, to some, I was still that pitcher, still the guy playing away from the unthinkable, and I suppose they weren't entirely wrong.

I liked to think of it as playing toward something wonderful. As reaching for something remarkable. As living the life I got instead of the one I'd assumed. The fact it also put another day between the monster and me wasn't entirely insignificant either. Another game. Another four at bats. I was an outfielder, just a guy trying to make his way separating the fastballs from the sliders. But, generally, when I walked into a room, a ghost followed.

"He was the sure thing," Chipper Jones recounted to reporters late on that Friday night one October. "The next *guy*."

That ghost.

Chipper was in that ballpark, in that batter's box, a decade and six days before. Then he was a teammate for a couple months in 2010, which made me an Atlanta Brave for a couple months, just like I'd allowed myself to dream when my friend Dennis and I had played catch in the backyard forever ago. The Braves had traded for me in August, we were in the playoffs—not Chipper, he'd blown out his knee—that October, and Bobby Cox was retiring, and we were all in San Francisco to play the Giants, one last run for the Braves the way I remembered them. And me.

Me. I was five years into the accumulation of at bats, all those I'd lost when I was busy being a pitcher, then forgetting how to be a pitcher, and then trying to become a pitcher again. I was a year removed from being a St. Louis Cardinal, they having seen my batting average fall from .285 to .264 to .231 over three seasons, and then a young Colby Rasmus had arrived to take innings in center field, along with at bats. I knew I was done in St. Louis long before it was over, as my playing time had slipped and my batting average with it, or perhaps it was the other way around. I was unhappy at the end. Tony had to know it. Free agency was coming after 2009, and when the Cardinals were swept by the Dodgers in the division series, I packed for home and another fresh start.

I signed with the Kansas City Royals for a year, which became all of twenty-seven games when I pulled a quadriceps muscle, and got back just in time to hit .367 in the week before the July 31 trade deadline.

Rusty Kuntz, an amazingly talented coach for the Royals, leaned into the batting cage one afternoon a few minutes before the deadline. In a game in which coaches sometimes were more concerned with themselves and their careers, Rusty thought first of what was best for the player. The game was hard. Rusty knew it. He was selfless and genuine in his teachings, in his support, and in the energy he brought to the grind. He was a guy the players would say "gets it," meaning he knows what allows ballplayers to perform and produce. As important, he knows what pulls them apart. And it's all separated by about an inch.

"Hey, player," he said, talking to me, "you need to go to the manager's office."

"What for?" I asked.

"All I can tell you," he said with a grin, "is it's not good for me."

Among his other duties, Rusty was the outfield coach.

"Am I getting traded?"

He shrugged. "Manager's office."

I laid my bat against the netting. When I reached the office, Ned Yost, who had replaced Trey Hillman after 35 games, was there. So was the general manager, Dayton Moore.

"Hey," Ned said, "you've been traded."

"OK."

"To the Braves," he finished. "It's really a good thing. They need you."

The Braves. My Braves. Like the baseball gods had shone a light on me. All the unhappiness—I hadn't gotten along with Hillman, the injury, the losing, in all a situation that hadn't agreed with me—cleared in the moment Ned said, "Braves."

They were in first place in the NL East. They were a team. The first time I went to dinner as a Brave, I looked around and was surrounded by twenty teammates. Bobby Cox, the legendary manager, would retire at the end of the year, and I'd get to watch his farewell. Now I just had to hit.

The ball flew off my bat sometimes. I hit 11 home runs in 6 weeks in '07, when every at bat drew wild and comforting cheers from Cardinals fans, then 25 home runs in 120 games in '08. Other times, just putting the bat on the ball was an effort, like I was forever a half step behind, forever seeking the answer in the cage.

I was still in there fighting when the air went cool that October, and the Braves were still in it, and it was game two of the National League Division Series at AT&T Park, and we were all out there in the eleventh inning, waiting on the swing that would end it. I arrived at the plate, looking for a fastball in the form of a taco.

The pitcher was Ramón Ramírez, a right-handed reliever. As I'd measured Ramírez from the on-deck circle, our catcher, Brian McCann, had hissed at me. He'd flied out against Ramirez in the tenth inning.

"His glove, Ank," he said. "When he's comin' with the heater, he squeezes his glove. Looks like a taco."

I nodded. A taco. OK.

Ramírez came set. And I'm thinking to myself, *That a taco? Yeah, that could be a taco maybe.*

I fouled it off.

He threw me five fastballs. The last one was definitely a taco. It landed in the bay.

I had to resist the urge to return immediately to the dugout. Running the bases seemed redundant. I wanted to go laugh with the guys on the top step. I wanted to tell 'em about that fastball, how I was looking for it, barreled it, and knocked forty-four thousand people on their butts.

Instead, after a muted bat flip, an ex-pitcher's bat flip, whatever you might call it, I hightailed it around the bases and went straight to McCann.

"Taco," I said, laughing.

"Taco!" he shouted.

I didn't know how long this would last, honestly. I was just thirty-one. I felt young. I could still run. I could throw. Man, could I throw a baseball. Not confined to an imaginary box and an umpire's interpretation of it, I was free again, and the ball behaved again. I loved to throw.

Hitting was hard.

That fifth fastball split the plate, a little up. The contact was so pure I could barely feel the ball off the bat. The right fielder, Nate Schierholtz, made a few disheartened strides toward the brick wall behind him. No ballpark can hold a 450-foot fly ball. And that one landed in the bay.

And so I don't recall being happier on a baseball field than I was that October night in San Francisco, the night I struck the blow to win a ball game for those guys, wearing the uniform I'd so admired for as long as I could remember. I was a ballplayer. A good ballplayer. A struggling ballplayer at times, a great one given the moment. But, all in all, a ballplayer. No more, no less. How often over the years I'd hoped just for that.

"You know, it's awesome," Chipper said that night. "It really is, how things come full circle. He's had the bad taste in his mouth for so long. Trust me, I was in the batter's box against him and it's not fun. But he's here, back in the playoffs and a hero for the Braves tonight."

Yeah, you know, something like that.

CHAPTER
TWENTY-EIGHT

Harvey Dorfman died during spring training, my first with the Washington Nationals, in 2011.

He would have explained this better. That is, what happened to me. What happens to all of us. How a grown man who has performed a single act his entire life, an act that is so simple or has become so simple, finds that it becomes not simple and, beyond that, in a lot of ways, incapacitating.

I couldn't remember how to throw a baseball. What it felt like. Did I bring my arm back like this? Or like this? What would my wrist do? Bent? Straight? Where would I hold the ball in my hand? Did I let go of it now? Or . . . now?

Then, of course, it was too late, and then every minute on a baseball field became devoted to throwing a damned strike, and then so did the rest of my life. It wasn't healthy. In fact, it got pretty dark some days.

He also could have explained what came after that, when the clouds lifted and when I was me again. We met that afternoon in the spring of 2000, we became inseparable a year later, and after that he became the friend I needed. It wasn't just me either. So many times conversations with other ballplayers, other young men, some lost and others found, started "Hey, you're a Harvey guy, right?" We'd recall his go-to musings, chuckle at the Harveyisms, and then get to reciting the virtues of Harvey. He saved careers. He probably saved lives, or at least made them exceedingly more livable. The world was simpler from where he sat, and he was wise enough and kind enough to make a little room for the rest of us who wouldn't otherwise see it like that. We were all Harvey guys.

"So what are you gonna do about it, Ank?" That's what he'd say, and I'd come up with something, and then I'd go do that, with Harvey's help.

He was seventy-five and very ill when I set out from Jupiter, Florida, one morning to see him. He was in Asheville, North Carolina, at home, where more and more he was bedridden. Over the previous decade, he'd become part of the fabric of my daily life, from the day Scott Boras introduced him to me to when he became my shrink—"I don't shrink, I stretch," he'd protest—to when he became what I'd hoped for in a father and what my boys should've had in a grandfather. I had to see him. Declan was a newborn, and when I called Harvey to tell him I was coming, he rasped, "I'm only still breathing to see the pictures."

The plan that day was to fly into Atlanta and connect into Asheville. There were storms, and the second flight was canceled, so Lory and I rented a car and drove the two hundred miles to Harvey's house. I wanted her to meet him. The final hour, we drove in darkness and a heavy downpour as we ascended into the Great Smoky Mountains. *Harvey lives on the top of a mountain*, I thought while squinting through the rain and windshield wipers. *Of course he does.*

Harvey knew he was dying. I knew he was dying. I went to say thank you.

Before Harvey, I'd not given much thought to the reasons certain people come along and become part of who you are. So many had come and gone already. So few had stuck. Yeah, Harvey was paid by Scott Boras to settle the fluttering souls of the .220 hitters and gopher-balling pitchers out there, but that wasn't why he answered his phone at 3 o'clock in the morning "Ank, you all right?" It wasn't why he stayed on the phone until the morning turned orangey-gray up in those mountains, until my heart was settled and my eyes were dry.

Harvey was well enough to come to the table for dinner. We talked about nothing, really, the way old friends do when the weather's bad, the house is warm, and the food—his wife, Anita, cooked—is comforting.

I'd turned my back on my father because I was a better person without him. But I also knew I'd have Harvey. He'd tell me it wasn't my fault. I was not responsible for who—more precisely, what—my father was, or what he'd done to my mother and me, or what I should have done about it. Sometimes I believed him. But it did soften the guilt I carried. I could not have changed what happened on the mound that day in St. Louis or in the years that followed, not by trying harder or caring more.

What happened happened. Now what?

By then, I was proud of whom I'd become. In a lot of ways, I felt like I was a survivor. I liked the way I looked in Harvey's eyes. More, I liked what that said about me. It was important to me to sit across from Harvey a different man, a better one. That was why I went. To say good-bye, of course. But also to show him he'd led me to a good place. I was OK.

I couldn't say much on his doorstep the next morning. We both knew there'd be one last hug, one last sad smile.

"Thank you, Harvey," I said. "Thank you."

Not long after, we spoke on the phone. He was tired. He told me he'd pinned a photo of Declan on the wall so he could see him.

"It's going to be OK," he said.

"Harvey . . . " I started.

He stopped me.

"*You*," he said. "*You* are going to be OK."

"I know, Harvey."

"Know what else?"

"What?"

"It's not your fault."

I laughed. So did he.

Harvey died a few days later.

So you want to know about the yips? About the monster? Harvey knew the yips. He knew they weren't temporary. He knew they weren't confined to a ball field. And he knew there'd be casualties, starting with me. He was right all along, by the way. He was saving my life. Perhaps not in the literal way, because, as I've told my friends, "You ever find me hanging from the garage rafters, I was murdered." It wasn't that way.

I saved the life I had, though, the one I wouldn't have given up for anything. Harvey showed me how, sometimes simply by asking, "OK, what the fuck you gonna do about it?" Emphasis on the profanity, hard like that, as if to say, *It's a big-boy world out there, Ank, and bad stuff happens, and then you decide: I'm in or I'm out.* I answered that question every day, every damned day, and in the end I was prouder of that than I was the home runs and the strikeouts and the money and even the uniform. What the fuck was I going to do about it? Win. Work. Try. Show up. Laugh. Cry. Fight if I had to. I was going to stand up to the big-boy world, all of it, and they could carry me away if that was what it came to. Maybe I couldn't always throw a strike. Maybe I couldn't always hit the slider. But sometimes I could.

"Yeah, I was watchin', Ank," he'd say. "I was watchin'. And I'm proud'a ya."

CHAPTER
TWENTY-NINE

I retired again, for good, shortly after the summer of '13, when the New York Mets released me and the phone went silent. I was thirty-three years old, coming up on thirty-four. More than eight years (and three thousand plate appearances) had passed between retirements. Lory and I had two young sons. They would grow up in a stable, loving household, not far from where I'd grown up. My mom lived with me. My father I'd lost track of. I fished for a while, raised my boys, and helped Lory do all the things she'd done alone for so long.

At the end, I'd thrown 242 innings and won 13 games in the major leagues. I'd played 4,115 innings in the outfield and retired a .240 hitter with 76 home runs. I arrived at twenty years old, departed a month before my thirty-fourth birthday, those fourteen years maybe not entirely what I'd expected but all I had, and I am proud of those years. All in all, I'd played for six teams in six cities—St. Louis, Kansas City, Atlanta, Washington, Houston, and finally New York. Some of those places loved me, others weren't sure what to do with me, and they all gave me countless opportunities for the life I wanted. Somewhere between the rage and the hopelessness, between the imperfect and the thrilling, between the ball in my hand and the bat on my shoulder, I did find the life I got. It was worth the time. It was worth the effort. It was never boring.

Seven years a pitcher, seven years not, a career spent on the fine line between glory and disaster, on the barrel of a bat, on the run and in pursuit, led me back to the same question. Not why, but why not? Why the hell not?

I wasn't exactly finished with baseball, but it seemed finished with me. I mourned that for a while, but nothing too crippling. After a year and a half out of the game, a year and a half chasing Declan, Ryker, and whatever fish was biting, and pushing my boat farther across the ocean for the big fish, I took a job with the Washington Nationals. They asked me to be their life skills coordinator, a vague title for a vague job. I guessed I'd be the guy who, no matter the problem, could look a player in the eye and say, "Yeah, been there," and then, perhaps channeling Harvey, add, "So what are you gonna do about it?" And in the process of looking a young and troubled man in the eye, and listening to his story, and feeling the pain he'd been hiding for too long, I began to remember who I was. That was me.

I met Domenick Mancini for breakfast at a place called Jimmies, which stood just off the first tee at Turtle Creek Golf Club and served the dual purposes of restaurant and "baseball gallery." It was mid-June 2015. I came from Jupiter, a drive of about ninety minutes up I-95. We were ten minutes from the Nationals' spring training complex, where for the previous four months Domenick had worked very hard, even desperately, to throw a baseball so it would go where he intended.

He was twenty-one years old, same as I was on October 3, 2000.

We sat at a small table on the patio, which was crowded. The waitress twisted sideways to navigate the gap between our table and the one beside ours, where a woman and her young son worked over a floppy stack of pancakes. Golfers scuffed past on the path between the patio and the golf course.

Dom was maybe six foot three and lean. He'd been drafted the previous June from Miami Dade Junior College. The Nationals had taken him in the twelfth round and signed him for $150,000, nearly twice what twelfth-rounders typically received. That was because of the 97 mph fastball. He had a big arm. Everybody loves those. He fell to the twelfth round because he'd suffered a minor injury near the end of his final college season, and he wasn't always sure where that fastball would end up, and the scouts didn't know either, so the debate over one Domenick Mancini, right-handed pitcher, was whether that fastball was hard enough and close enough to controllable to save him from a very short professional career.

After I hung up my cleats and was coaching with the Nationals, I met many young men like Dom. More than I expected. They didn't all have the yips. Some did. Some felt it coming and wore expressions like men paddling back from a waterfall. Others were finding themselves casualties of pro ball—the pressure to perform, to grow up, to justify their signing bonuses, to make their families and hometowns proud, to stand up under the scouting reports, to make the right decisions, to be accountable for the bad ones. Social media recorded their triumphs and predicted they'd rocket through the minors. It also recorded their mistakes. Then, when they were done with all that, they were asked to hit .350. Or strike out the side. Maybe learn a new pitch. Change the way they've swung the bat for fifteen years. That against the sort of competition they'd never seen before, both in the other dugouts and in their own clubhouse. To an eighteen-year-old in A ball who has thirty pounds to gain and what must seem like an entirely new sport to learn, the major leagues might never have been so far away. That's a lot to forget every night.

It does things to people, especially young ones. They start failing at baseball for the first time in their lives. Doubts gather and gain strength. Sometimes those things send a baseball to the backstop when it was supposed to hit a catcher's mitt.

That morning at Jimmies, Dom was composed. He smiled when he talked and even laughed at his own expense. He said he might be in a little trouble as far as his career was concerned, and I told him I understood how that felt. He said when he drove around town he sometimes slowed at Little League fields and watched young boys and girls throw baseballs so easily, so accurately, and wished he could again too, and I told him I'd once hit the backstop with a ceremonial first pitch at my old Little League and been booed for it. He said there were good days and bad and admitted they were mostly bad lately. I nodded my encouragement, but what I thought was *He's in the thick of it.*

I was a life skills coordinator, which is what they called a sports psychologist who doesn't have a college degree but has seen plenty of time in the thick of it. It's what they called the guy who knew too well the doubts swimming in Domenick's heart and head. Where they'd send him. How they'd probably never leave. But you fight. You find a way through it or around it. You ask for help. They send me in. And we go to breakfast.

Dom grew up in Weston, Florida, outside Fort Lauderdale. His father, Sal, was a pretty fair baseball player in high school and loved the game. By the time Dom was two years old, Sal was feeding him tennis balls to knock across the living room, and while other sports came and went through Dom's adolescence, his game was always going to be baseball. He became a pitcher at ten years old. He made his high school team as a freshman, grew three or four inches and added twenty pounds between his sophomore and junior years, and by his senior year was throwing 92 mph. He won three games in the playoffs for American Heritage High School that spring and signed with Florida Atlantic University (FAU). For a young man whose goal—dream, even—was to be a professional baseball player, to one day pitch in the major leagues, the path was promising. He was big enough and strong enough and threw hard enough. All he had to do was get hitters out. All he had to do was throw strikes.

Dom did not pitch in an official game at FAU. He instead began to unravel at FAU.

"It wasn't one pitch," Dom said. "Just a gradual thing. So gradual. I got to FAU that summer, and I'd make one or two bad throws. I'd think, *That was weird*. In games that summer, I'd pitch fine. Then the semester started, and now I'm making three or four bad throws."

Dom got confused, started losing confidence, and pretty soon was reasonably sure he couldn't pitch at a Division I school in that condition. So he transferred to nearby Miami Dade. He'd pitch his way back to a four-year school in junior college. And he'd go back to playing catch with his father, Sal, at the park, where it had all started. They'd get their gloves. Dom would bring the bucket of balls. That's right. A bucket. Just to play catch.

He couldn't have his father chasing baseballs across the park. Even when his father backed up to a fence, the caroms were unpredictable (and occasionally dangerous), so they'd throw and throw and throw, and then they'd go find the balls and refill the bucket and start over. Dom came to hate the metallic *chunk*s, *ping*s, and *thud*s of baseballs running up against chain-link fences. He'd miss the clean and mindless pleasure of baseballs going where they were supposed to go, finding leather. But, you know, maybe the next throw would be the one that solved it. If not that one, then the one after. His mind would get out of the way eventually, he believed, and then hoped, and then he could get back to where all this had started—standing on a mound and throwing the pitches that would make him good enough.

Dom had some days like that too. He had some very good stretches at Miami Dade. The coaches there lowered his arm slot, and that worked for a time, until it didn't, so by the fall of 2013, Dom was seriously considering quitting baseball. He'd been out of high school for a year and a half. The struggle was so raw, so real, so hopeless that when the baseball team held its annual scout day, Dom sat in the stands with the scouts and charted pitches.

"Hey, Dom," a scout said. "You throwing today?"

"Not today," he answered.

"Why not?"

He shrugged.

As the day went on, Dom reconsidered. Why not? Back off a little, try that lower arm slot, throw a few fastballs, find out once and for all if he could do this. The scouts were all there. He might be done with baseball anyway. No regrets. So he threw.

And, well, he threw strikes. He started calling out locations, and that's where the ball would go. He felt a twinge of confidence. He smiled to himself between pitches, not having had even fifteen minutes like that since high school. The scouts pointed their radar guns and made notes on their clipboards.

One of those scouts told Dom later, "You looked good."

Dom thanked him and tried not to look surprised.

"Know how hard you were throwing?"

He shrugged. He knew he'd eased off the velocity for the sake of strikes.

"Eighty-nine?" Dom guessed.

"Ninety-six."

Ninety-six, and he'd commanded it. It had felt easy. That day, those throws, how he was able to walk off the mound with his head high, to feel joy, it allowed him to remember he'd been pretty good at pitching once. And that it was in there still. Maybe, he thought, he'd whipped it, and when the season came, he mostly pitched like he had for the scouts, carrying that confidence as far as he could, into the draft, through a summer of minor-league ball, and into a winter in which he'd never worked harder to become the best pitcher he could be.

A few months later, on the patio at Jimmies, Dom told that story. He'd allowed himself to believe that he was free from the anxiety, from the single imprecise throw that could lead to the emotional wobble that could kick over the first psychological domino that could—maybe, chillingly—take the game away. His game. That he was free from whatever he'd left back there.

He shook his head at the absurdity of it. The throws were going sideways again. It had started in the winter, when a few inches of gnawing imprecision had restarted the emotional ripples. The indecision. The way he'd draw back his arm and then go physically and intellectually blank. He'd fought it, yet he arrived at spring training uncomfortable, not quite right, afraid of what might come when everyone was watching.

First thing every morning, two lines of pitchers—one along the foul line, the other in the outfield—would begin their throwing routines. Dom grew anxious. His throws were getting wilder. He began to fear he'd accidentally bean a teammate. When everyone else was cutting up and shaking off the morning rust, he was trying to slow his heart rate and talk himself into relaxing. One morning, he showed up with a bucket filled with baseballs, and as he lugged it to the foul line, he wondered if he even liked baseball anymore. He was sure it didn't think much of him.

I'd given Dom my business card in spring training. He looked at it, saw the words *life coach*, and thought, *My life is fine.* Then he went to his hotel room and prayed they wouldn't ask him to throw the next day. A couple months later, after enough of those nights, he called.

"Now what?" he asked.

"Pancakes," I said.

I told him we'd figure it out, though I wasn't sure. I told him to have fun, to remember what it felt like to be care-free on a baseball field. I told him my story in ten minutes, starting with that pitch in St. Louis, ending with the day I retired from pitching. I used some of Harvey Dorfman's words, but really I borrowed from his understanding over our breakfasts. I could talk to Dom while we played catch. In the days that followed, I did. And I could walk him through the techniques that had once lowered my anxiety levels so I could cope with my relationship with the base-ball. I did. One pitch at a time, I told him. Just that one. Not the last one, not the next one, the one in your hand. But this, in the end, would be between Dom and Dom.

As we finished out on the patio, the woman at the table next to ours asked if we were ballplayers. Dom said we were. She put her hand on her son's shoulder—he was maybe five or six years old—and said he was a big baseball fan. She asked if we had any advice for him.

Dom smiled at me and then at her.

"Hey, just have fun," he said. "Don't take it too seriously."

I grinned.

"Yeah," I said, "that's pretty much it."

She thanked us. When she turned to go, Dom looked at me and said, "Man, I sorta wish I was that kid."

A couple weeks later, Dom was in the locker room. He watched three teammates walk into the manager's office, one at a time, and return having been released.

"Hey, Dom," one of the coaches said, "we gotta talk to you for a sec."

Damn, Dom thought, *this is it.*

He walked in. Michael Barrett, the former big-league catcher, sat behind a desk. Three or four pitching coaches stood nearby.

"Dom," Barrett said, "we chose to release you."

He said some other stuff. Probably it was kind, reassuring Dom there'd be other chances out there for him. Dom didn't hear much after the "release" part, because he was so relieved he wouldn't have to throw that day.

Dom returned to his hotel room. He had a three-hour drive ahead of him. Before that, however, he sat on the bed and, on a pad of paper, wrote down everything wonderful he'd experienced in baseball. The rest of his life waited, and he didn't want to forget. When he finished, he found that the list was longer than he'd expected. He put the pad in a backpack, put the backpack on his shoulder, and went to his car.

Dom reenrolled at FAU. He majored in business management with a minor in finance. He was due to graduate in spring 2017.

"I'm OK," he told me later. "I put in the work. I don't sit here and think I blew it."

"Sometimes it just doesn't get fixed."

Maybe, he said, he'd pick up a baseball in a few months, go to the park, see if his dad didn't want to have a catch. You never know, he said. You never know. And if not, that's what the bucket was for.

When breakfast was over, Dom shook my hand.

"Hey, Dom," I said.

"Yeah."

"It's not your fault."

"I know, Ank."

"Stay in touch."

I supposed I'd try to push some of Harvey's teachings into a new generation of players, of men. I supposed I could offer a fractured career, a crazy career, a career I am resolutely proud of, and a life that I like to think of as highly textured as credential enough.

I did that for a year, and I still get phone calls and e-mails from people stricken with fear and uncertainty. And I tell them it's not their fault. We start there.

So very few people actually got it. Fewer still knew how to help. And there was only one Harvey. We didn't slay the monster together, but we stood shoulder to shoulder and tried. Then we bandaged up and got on our feet and tried again. Some days, we had our pick of monsters. We had our pick of venues. We had our pick of reasons. Of the whys.

The spring of 2001, months after I'd thrown a few pitches to the backstop in St. Louis and so ended one life and started another, my Little League called. Opening day was coming. Would I come? The kids would be so happy, the lady said. I drove to Sportsman's Park in Port St. Lucie, where I'd been handed my first real uniform, and discovered there could be a place where I felt safe. The old bleachers were filled. Colorful plastic flags draped the chain-link fences. I stood near the mound and waved, the ex–Little Leaguer turned big leaguer, feeling happy to be among them and totally unnerved by having to throw out the ceremonial first pitch. I couldn't say no. I wanted to. I couldn't.

I looked toward the backstop. There, behind the plate, stood a kid, maybe ten years old, in full catcher's gear, which hung from him like a tarp. He squatted, very serious.

Well, I thought, *this could be embarrassing.* I could do a lot of damage from sixty feet, six inches. Imagine what could happen from forty-six feet.

So, with a smile, I took a couple steps closer, wound up, and flipped the ball toward the kid in the man-sized catcher's gear. Underhanded.

The crowd booed.

There was a night in Houston during my final season that I think about still. Harvey was gone. I was living the career that maybe I hadn't wanted, but it was the one I got. I was living the life I wanted. I was satisfied, other than perhaps with the strikeouts. I was still working to be a hitter.

The Astros weren't very good. In fact, we were on our way to losing 111 games. I'd be released after 24 of those losses. Before I was, however, we were getting beat pretty good the night after we'd been beat worse. We were running out of pitchers. The bullpen was wrung out. Another game was over but for the final score, and there was tomorrow to think about, and the next day.

Bo Porter, our rookie manager, was desperate.

"Ank," he said.

I looked up.

He nodded toward the mound. "Can you give me anything?"

Porter seemed a good man. A solid baseball man. He'd been around the game forever, maybe even seen his share of cases like mine.

"You serious?" I asked.

"I'm serious," he said.

I was not stunned, exactly, but surprised. I didn't do that anymore. More than that, I couldn't do it anymore.

"Bo," I said as the whipping continued in front of us, "I would have to go to winter ball and pitch. And pitch. That's not as easy as it looks, to just go out there and jump on the mound. Not for anybody. And especially not for me."

I wanted to be a team guy. I didn't want to let him down. This, though, I just couldn't.

He shrugged. "I had to ask."

I sat on the bench and watched the final couple innings. *Even the people in the game*, I thought, *have no idea what this is about.*

Just pick up the ball and throw it, Rick. C'mon, Rick. Just throw it. How hard can it be?

Had I blown out my shoulder, they'd get it. If there were a scar, a medical report, an X-ray, then maybe they'd get it. Could I have restarted, stood again on a mound, retaken a bygone fastball and the courage to throw it? Maybe.

But at what cost? So the nightmares could return? So I could spend my days drowning, burying, denying, and fighting again? So I could summon the monster? Get a rematch? Best two out of three?

No.

I had the life I wanted. It was this one. I'd make the best of that.

EPILOGUE

Going on fifteen years after I'd completely fouled up that playoff game along with my career—and, it seemed for a long time after that, my life—my phone rang, a 314 area code, so St. Louis. A man named Joe Pfeiffer was on the line. Joe was in corporate sales and ran the fantasy baseball camps for the Cardinals. I liked Joe.

"What's up?" I greeted him.

"Hey, Ank," he said.

Joe asked about the family, life down in Jupiter, my golf game, whether the fish were biting. Good, good, depends on the day, and occasionally, I reported.

"So Ank . . . ," he said.

"Yeah, Joe," I said.

"Come throw out a first pitch," he said. "You think maybe?"

Joe was asking me to throw a pregame ceremonial first pitch at Busch Stadium, a topic he'd raised before. The job entailed having your name announced, waving to a full ballpark, walking to the pitcher's mound, standing on that pitcher's mound, maybe waving again, then throwing a baseball sixty feet, six inches to a man crouched behind home plate. Wave again, shake the catcher's hand, go home. That's about it. I was going to be in St. Louis anyway, he figured, signing autographs at Busch Stadium. Chris Carpenter, who'd won 144 regular-season baseball games as a pitcher, 95 for the Cardinals, not including the 10 more he'd won in the playoffs (3 in the World Series), had once told me he'd never been more nervous than he was while throwing out a ceremonial first pitch. I hadn't forgotten that conversation.

"Joe . . . ," I said.

"Fans would love to see you again, Ank," Joe said.

"Joe . . . "

"I know."

Truth was, I would've loved to see them too. I'd been a Royal, a Brave, a National, an Astro, and a Met. I was a Cardinal in my soul, where it mattered. I still felt special in St. Louis and in that ballpark, because both had accepted me in sickness and in health, and those kinds of bonds stay bonds forever, especially in baseball-mad St. Louis.

But of course I couldn't do it.

"No, Joe. Sorry."

Joe was a good man. The request was more than reasonable. And it wasn't even so much a request as it was a friendly offer. I'd left St. Louis and the Cardinals after the

2009 season, but I would remain one of them, no matter the uniform, no matter that I had retired four years later and would in time take that job with the Nationals. I still hoped to represent the spirit of the place, which would remember me as the young man who'd failed so spectacularly and the slightly older man who'd returned when maybe no one else could've. It didn't hurt when that was pretty spectacular too.

I was the pitcher who'd contracted the yips at about the worst possible time, spent nearly five years fighting that with a determination that bordered on obsession, and turned up the hitter who could put a ball in the top deck and the outfielder whose arm was again golden. It was all so marvelous and strange and, to the folks in St. Louis, damned lovable, so, yeah, bring back Rick Ankiel and put him up on that humpbacked stage so they could show him again how they would forever honor his courage.

It's just . . . I wouldn't. I couldn't.

"Thanks, Joe. How about this: I throw it from center field?"

I laughed. He laughed.

"One day maybe," I said. "See ya, Joe."

"Take care, Ank."

I thumbed off the phone.

It doesn't go away. Not with time or age, not with a change in job description, not even with a decade of not really having to think about it anymore. Not in retirement. Not for Wiffle Ball in the backyard. Not for a ceremony. Not because, aw, hell, it's just a sixty-foot toss; how hard could that be?

Honestly, it's *really* hard.

I'd have to practice that throw. A lot. I'd have to stand in my backyard across from some other guy wearing a glove, a ball in my hand, and conjure tens of thousands of people watching, waiting for me to make that throw from the top of a freshly raked mound to the pocket of a ceremonial catcher's shiny mitt. I'd have to live that throw over and over, feel my stomach coil and hear the blood being drawn from my head, to create those things from nothing but the sound of my breath in my own backyard before I could know I was ready for that city and that ball-park again.

I held the phone for a time and thought I could prob-ably pull off that pitch, given time. I could still smile in the face of anxiety, the casual way I carried myself to por-tray *I don't give a fuck*, so nobody would have to know that this would be hard. I could muscle something passable across sixty feet of trampled grass, probably. Sure, I could, I thought.

Oh, but what if I couldn't? What if the dumbest and most meaningless throw ever—the one city councilmen and heads of sales departments and pop singers and den mothers make in hundreds of major- and minor-league ballparks every night—what if mine went to the backstop?

I finally let go of his call, but the conversation gnawed at me. I hadn't had to consider the monster in so long. I hadn't had to confront it. I'd often said, when asked, that I'd be afflicted forever, that it sat right here—and I'd tap the place on my shoulder where people carry their fears and burdens—and that it had a permanent home there.

But, gone from the game, out from under the microscope, away from the questions and the what-the-hell stares, the monster was irrelevant and therefore likely restless, so off to seep into the skull of some other unsuspecting mope who'd rear back and make a perfectly ordinary throw and think, *Huh. That didn't feel quite right.*

A year passed. My sons grew. Those young men I spoke to, the ones who were sure they were going to be big-league pitchers and yet could not bear to throw a pitch, drew up the nerve to make pitches anyway and live with whatever dusty result followed.

I grew too. My mother was helping to raise my boys. I liked to listen to her read to them and tell stories about her father, who'd given me my name and my eyes. Mom and I had some rough patches, as the years of drama—in the house, on those baseball fields, within the family— had served to push us apart. Maybe I simply could not bear her pain along with mine. Maybe she reminded me I should've done more than I had. I should've protected her. I should've tried. Now she cooked for the boys and sang them funny songs that sounded familiar, like something out of a childhood I'd buried a long time before. She'd get this do-over, this chance in the peace of a house that would not fall down around her. I was happy for that, happy for her. Probably it hadn't been the life she wanted, and I remembered how that could wear on a person. She'd suffered more than one heart attack in her later years and, waiting on a new kidney, three times a week underwent dialysis. Even in the worst of it, she was present for De-clan and Ryker, the lives she got. Sometimes I'd loved her desperately for trying so hard, and sometimes I'd wondered why she hadn't tried harder, and usually I'd just tried to survive on my own. I liked that we had a chance to live some of those years over, as much as we could, or at least live them better.

It wasn't her fault. It wasn't mine either.

A man I hardly knew asked if I'd come to Springfield, Missouri, sign some autographs, meet some clients, throw a first pitch at a minor-league game, and make a few thousand dollars. It was the summer of 2015. Something they called the Mobil Super Baseball Tour was passing through town. A decade before I'd had 136 at bats for the Springfield Cardinals on my way back to the major leagues, about half at Hammons Field. I knew the place. I knew the people a little.

Before I said no, I thought about the players I counseled. How many I'd told there was no trick to beating this thing, and hell, there might be no beating it at all, but there was no shame in trying. Trying was the only way to find out. Trying required courage. Trying meant allowing for failure. Trying was hard and lonely. So yeah, I recommended trying.

I thought about Harvey. What would Harvey say? "Go on, Ank, what the fuck"? Or, maybe, "What's the point, Ank? What do you have left to prove? Don't do it for the money. Don't do it for any reason except that you want to."

I told the guy sure, I'd see him in Springfield.

They set up a table in an auto-supply store, somewhere between the oil filters and Turtle Wax. There was a DJ. I signed some autographs. Not a lot of people showed up, so I talked to the employees and hummed along to the music and thought a little about that night. My pitch.

You'll be fine, I assured myself. *Just one pitch. You can do this. Right? Just pick up the ball and throw it.*

Hammons Field is redbrick and green steel and minor-league charming. A long time before, it seemed, I'd spent some nights there sorting between the fastballs and the sliders and the cutters that would be part of my new life as a hitter. I'd run that outfield. I'd returned to that clubhouse on every one of those nights feeling four or five at bats closer to the big leagues, those same four or five at bats further out in front of the Thing. It couldn't catch me there. Couldn't touch me in the batter's box.

A man greeted me, told me his name, thanked me for coming, and handed me a glove. Absently accepting it, I asked, "What's this for?"

"We figured," he said, "you might want to *catch* the first pitch."

I smiled and handed it back.

The clubhouse was beyond the right-field fence. Beside the clubhouse, in a structure the size of a small warehouse, minor leaguers toiled in batting cages. The sound of batting practice, young men searching for perfect swing paths and then lives in the big leagues, echoed in my head. About a hundred people, many in Cardinals shirts and caps, gathered around buffet tables in what I assumed to be a sponsors' event. Some glanced over, and I saw that they recognized me, and they returned to their plates of fried chicken and coleslaw.

A net had been strung into which batters hit baseballs from a tee. A bucket of baseballs was nearby. I took one of those balls and tossed it ten feet into the net. Then another. And another. I looked over to where the party was breaking up. A few of the folks had stopped eating and socializing and were watching this curiosity of the guy who was going to be Koufax psyching himself up for a single pitch that wouldn't count. I heard the ceremony beginning and walked across the field to the dugout. The team's catcher introduced himself.

"I'm throwing a knuckler," I said. "If you miss it, you owe me five bucks."

He looked at me and laughed.

"Seriously," I said.

We walked out together. The PA announcer introduced me. I waved on my way across the infield, climbed the dirt mound, and set my left foot parallel to the rubber. I could almost hear the mound whisper, "Ah, the prodigal son . . . " The catcher squatted behind the plate. I looked in.

Who cares, man? Nobody cares what happens here. You're telling all those kids to go face their demons. So go face yours. Here you are. Can you feel the ball in your hand? Yes, you can. Can you throw a baseball sixty feet? Yes, you can. Does it scare the shit out of you? Hell, yes.

All right, Rick, right foot back . . .

My heart fluttered. Something heavy landed in my stomach. I was nervous but in control. I could see the people and hear them. The blood stayed in my head, where it belonged.

Nothing could ever be as bad as some of those days were, back then. So I wouldn't fight this. I'd allow it to make me feel afraid, and so feel alive. I'd swing that sword. I'd never, ever find something that would put me back in a big-league ball game. It doesn't exist. But I could do this. I could throw this one pitch and live with the result. If the people laughed, they laughed. If they cheered, I'd be good with that too. If the ball hit the backstop, hey, somebody would just go pick it up.

Who the hell cares, right, Harv?

I exhaled. I gripped the ball. I drew back my arm and strode with my right leg and, stiff-wristed, threw that knuckleball. Over those sixty feet, six inches, that ball flew, and paused, and wobbled, and caught a gust, and found its way, appropriately.

It was a strike. Or, hell, close enough. The people cheered. They probably would've no matter what. But they cheered. And I waved.

ACKNOWLEDGMENTS

We would like to express our gratitude to those who helped turn this book from a light conversation over a beer (or two) in Jupiter, Florida into something we hope is very special. We believed the world could use another story with a happy ending. It doesn't happen without our wives, Lory Ankiel and Kelly Brown, their patience and love and wisdom. Start there.

It also doesn't happen without Rick's mom, Denise, who summoned memories she'd rather have left behind.

Thank you to those who similarly gave of their time and perspectives: Tony La Russa, Dave Duncan, Gary Bennett, Steve Blass, Scott Boras, Mike Fiore, Domenick Mancini, Mike Matheny, Johnny DiPuglia, Tony Malizia, Kurt Schloagle, Ken Ravizza, and Mark Oakley.

Thanks to the folks at David Black Agency, beginning with David Black and Jenny Herrera. And at PublicAffairs, especially Ben Adams, Collin Tracy, and Connie Oehring, whose belief in the book was inspiring and whose expertise in putting it together was imperative.

Thanks, too, to the folks at Yahoo! Sports. Fellow baseball writer Jeff Passan covered for Tim on plenty of mornings. And evenings. Some afternoons. We're grateful. Thanks to Bob Condor, Johnny Ludden, Marcus Vanderberg and Joe Garza for their support.

Thanks to Tyler Beckstrom, who put Rick and Tim together at the start. To the St. Louis Cardinals' public relations staff—Brian Bartow, Melody Yount, and Chris Tunno. To Jim Trdinich of the Pittsburgh Pirates and Amanda Comack of the Washington Nationals.

Thanks to Phillip Kennedy, Eric Jenks, Don Carman, and Guy McCuen.

Rick Ankiel was a major-league pitcher and outfielder with the St. Louis Cardinals and Washington Nationals, among other teams, for eleven seasons. Born in 1979, Ankiel debuted with the Cardinals a month after his twentieth birthday and became the first major-league player since Babe Ruth to win at least ten games as a pitcher and hit at least fifty home runs. He retired as a player in 2013. He is employed as the Nationals' life skills coordinator. With his wife, Lory, and sons Declan and Ryker, Ankiel lives in Jupiter, Florida.

Tim Brown is an award-winning writer with twenty-five years' experience covering Major League Baseball at the *Los Angeles Times*, the *Newark Star-Ledger*, the *Cincinnati Enquirer*, the *Los Angeles Daily News*, and Yahoo! Sports. He cowrote, with Jim Abbott, the *New York Times* best seller *Imperfect: An Improbable Life*. He resides with his wife, Kelly, in Venice, California.

PublicAffairs is a publishing house founded in 1997. It is a tribute to the standards, values, and flair of three persons who have served as mentors to countless reporters, writers, editors, and book people of all kinds, including me.

I. F. STONE, proprietor of *I. F. Stone's Weekly*, combined a commitment to the First Amendment with entrepreneurial zeal and reporting skill and became one of the great independent journalists in American history. At the age of eighty, Izzy published *The Trial of Socrates*, which was a national bestseller. He wrote the book after he taught himself ancient Greek.

BENJAMIN C. BRADLEE was for nearly thirty years the charismatic editorial leader of *The Washington Post*. It was Ben who gave the *Post* the range and courage to pursue such historic issues as Watergate. He supported his reporters with a tenacity that made them fearless and it is no accident that so many became authors of influential, best-selling books.

ROBERT L. BERNSTEIN, the chief executive of Random House for more than a quarter century, guided one of the nation's premier publishing houses. Bob was personally responsible for many books of political dissent and argument that challenged tyranny around the globe. He is also the founder and longtime chair of Human Rights Watch, one of the most respected human rights organizations in the world.

.   .   .

For fifty years, the banner of Public Affairs Press was carried by its owner Morris B. Schnapper, who published Gandhi, Nasser, Toynbee, Truman, and about 1,500 other authors. In 1983, Schnapper was described by *The Washington Post* as "a redoubtable gadfly." His legacy will endure in the books to come.

Peter Osnos, *Founder and Editor-at-Large*